WEB AND DIGITAL FOR GRAPHIC DESIGNERS

Neil Leonard // Andrew Way // Frédérique Santune

BLOOMSBURY VISUAL ARTS
LONDON • NEW YORK • OXFORD • NEW DELHI • SYDNEY

BLOOMSBURY VISUAL ARTS
Bloomsbury Publishing Plc
50 Bedford Square, London, WC1B 3DP, UK
1385 Broadway, New York, NY 10018, USA

BLOOMSBURY, BLOOMSBURY VISUAL ARTS
and the Diana logo are trademarks of Bloomsbury
Publishing Plc

First published in Great Britain 2020

Cover design: Steve Stacey

A catalogue record for this book is available from
the British Library.

A catalogue record of this book is available from
the Library of Congress.

ISBN:
PB: 978-1-350-02755-8
ePDF: 978-1-350-02766-4
eBook: 978-1-350-02756-5

Typeset by Neil Leonard

Printed and bound in China

To find out more about our authors and books
visit www.bloomsbury.com and sign up for
our newsletters.

BANK Associates
Image over: The Berlin Studio of design agency,
BANK Associates.
www.bankassociates.de/

Contents

Introduction

The term 'graphic design' was coined in the 1920s. Since then, the profession has developed constantly, and nothing has encouraged and expedited this change more than the digital revolution.

Computers have existed for many years in various shapes and forms, but until the late 1970s and early 1980s, there was little need for graphic designers to pay any attention to them. Then, the graphic interface was born, and everything changed.

Many of the people that birthed the first graphic interfaces had knowledge, or experience of graphic design, and an interest in typography and image generation (Steve Jobs of Apple was perhaps the person who brought this consideration most prominently to computing and personal computers). These visionaries saw the need for crisp graphics, icon systems to guide users, typographic choices that communicated well and legibly on the screen, and the absolute need to make these important grey boxes desirable, well-designed objects.

Through, the 1980s, the Apple Mac brought new possibilities to the graphic design profession and made many time-consuming tasks, such as paste-up and typesetting, redundant overnight. While there has been some resurgence in these traditional ways of working, it is hard to imagine setting entire publications using letterpress now.

Around the same time as the rise of the Apple Mac, another development surfaced, and initially, many did not predict the way it would change graphic design forever.

The Internet has existed in some form since the Second World War, when it was used as a communication tool, but it wasn't until Sir Tim Berners Lee developed HTML (HyperText Markup Language) that the application and need for graphic designers to involve themselves in the Internet became clear.

HTML works in the same way as a traditional typesetter: a designer develops a set of rules and indicates which text or content should adhere to which rule; then, the typesetter styles the copy in the correct manner using the assigned style and typeface.

Similarly, HTML wraps areas of content in a way that allows graphic designers (or front-end developers, but we'll get on to that shortly) to write particular rules that govern its presentation.

The development of CSS (Cascading Style Sheets) meant that there were more possibilities open to designers, and it also meant that multiple pages could be managed from a central set of rules (a style sheet).

As connection speeds improved, the Internet began to host a greater range of content, from motion-based websites to applications and games. All of these areas require graphic designers, but all require a developed and specific skill set.

The number of ways digital content can be accessed has grown exponentially. Smartphones and tablet devices are able to access the Internet, and they are host to any number of applications and different forms of content. Designers play a vital part in the presentation and construction of this media.

As we move forward, there are limitless possibilities. It is impossible to predict which will take off, but all will involve elements of design, and specifically graphic design. Whether it is wearable tech, holograms, interactive installations, domotics or something we have not thought of yet, graphic designers will be there at the forefront.

In this book, we will explore these design roles and their development, and we will consider how this might shift in the future. We will offer an overview of the skills and attributes required to work in this exciting environment, and arm you with the tools, understanding and knowledge required to succeed. We will help you identify which visual communication skills you already possess, and which abilities you need to develop.

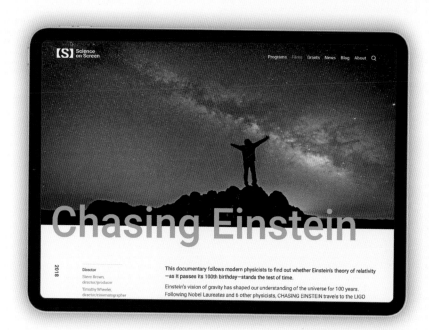

Amy Parker

Science on Screen

The online home for an arthouse theatre's popular film-and-lecture series, this site contains a database of films and programs going back to 2011. Amy's design brings together an exciting mix of contemporary digital design elements, from the use of web fonts to the layout achieved using a CSS grid.

www.amyhparker.com/projects/science-on-screen

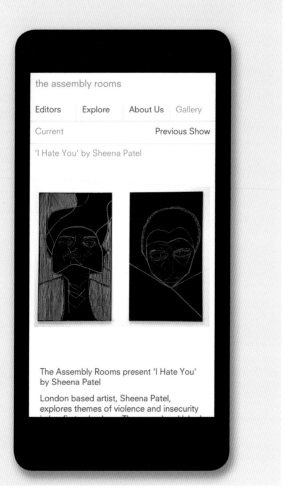

Planning Unit

The Assembly Rooms

Of the design, Planning Unit said 'our solution has been to craft a site that delivers content first, followed by subtle transitions, hinting at the craft employed by The Assembly Rooms.

Background video has been used to complement and reinforce the core proposition of editing through the site.' Planning Unit's design solution offers a rich experience for users, regardless of the device they are viewing the website on. Their layout adapts to screen sizes while keeping the grid-based motif consistent. The site utilises CSS properties such as transparencies, subtle fades and positioning of text above images to create an image-first navigation.

www.planningunit.co.uk/work/assembly-rooms/

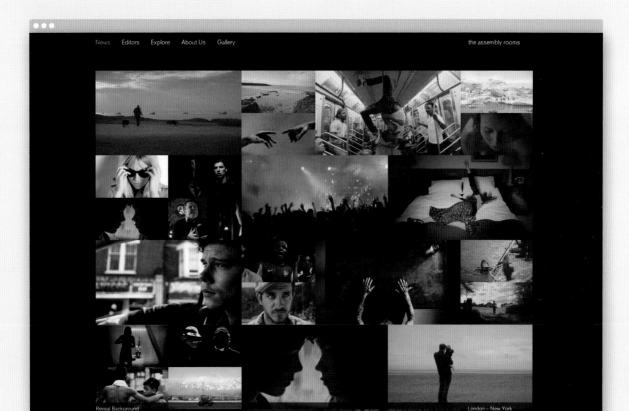

CHAPTER 1:
DESIGNING FOR DIGITAL

From the introduction of the Web, to anticipating what may come next, here we will consider what digital design is, and what it can be. This chapter will introduce you to the basic concepts that you need to understand before you start developing your interactive Web and digital projects. While digital and web-based design is a relatively recent profession when compared to that of print, we will explore the discipline's rich history and look at the design principles that will help you make the right aesthetic and functional decisions.

History of digital design

The range of tools designed to help graphic designers has grown greatly since the beginning of the twentieth century. From letterpress to photo composition, screen-printing to Letraset, technology consistently meant that the process of design could be realised by fewer people in less time than the previous studio incarnation. For more information on this journey, please check out the wonderful documentary *Graphic Means* by Bryar Levit.

The adoption of digital technology by the design industry was stratospheric, and in many ways, this led to wider use of these tools by people in associated industries, and users at home. A short time after Turing introduced the world to what is widely regarded as the first computer, great big processing machines were brought into a range of workplaces as a means of speeding up labour-intensive tasks, working through equations, and sometimes simply storing data.

While the industry was quick to react, the home equivalent – personal computers – did not catch on so fast. Largely, this slow uptake was due to the inaccessibility of the products as they generally required the user to know some programming languages in order to achieve the smallest task. However, this all changed when Apple introduced the Macintosh 128k personal desktop computer in 1984. The simple interface suddenly meant that these tools could be accessed by a great number of people, regardless of previous experience.

The launch of Apple Macintosh was successful, in part, because its creators treated the computer as a design object, not just a functional machine that processed data. The device had an attractive visual interface – the result of a suite of icons designed by Susan Kare and the attention that Steve Jobs paid to the system's typographic choices. As personal computers became more accessible, affordable, and developed capacity and processing power, so did the associated software packages. It was around this time that digital printing came into its own. Digital printing made it easier to print one-offs and to personalise communication, and digital scanning meant that high-resolution elements could be composited onto the page and adjusted with the suite of editing tools new to the market.

The story of developments in software packages is that of a series of start-ups, buyouts by big players, and mergers. Of the number of software developers that surfaced in the 1990s, only a handful of big players still remain and they largely control the means of digital production.

Alongside the development of software packages, bespoke operating systems were developed for the range of personal computers available in the market. Apple developed its iOS while Windows was the system used on the majority of machines (though other packages such as Linux were available).

The operating systems often came with bespoke office tools: for example, Windows came packaged with Microsoft Office, and Apple developed a cluster of programs under the iWork banner.

Pagemaker was one of the first software packages developed (in 1985) for document creation. It had a graphic interface that consisted of icons and options, which related to the process of physically mocking up a page – text boxes and font choices, for example.

QuarkXPress was one of the first packages that was developed (in 1987) specifically for designers, and it went to greater lengths to replicate the process of designing a document for print. The designer could import text and images onto

Apple Macintosh

Considered by many to be a design masterpiece, one might argue
that the Apple Macintosh launched the digital design revolution.
Now a common sight, this simple and elegant artefact brought
a computing interface into the houses and offices of many. This
computer democratised design and made possible processes that
once would have required the involvement of large teams.

a page, and then send a high-quality version of the layout to a printer, often as a PDF file. The package allowed for advances in typographic design and a greater range of layout tools; these tools led to the creation of expressive work that could not easily be achieved using analogue processes. The rise of interactive content, such as CD-ROMs and, eventually, online material, led to the development of packages that allowed both coders and visual designers to create content for these platforms easily.

Macromedia, founded in 1992, was one of the decade's larger companies developing software for designers. They released a suite of products that included tools for Web and print. They were perhaps best known for Dreamweaver, a package that allowed the designer to write markup code or use a graphical interface to adjust elements and generate code.

Another major innovation developed by Macromedia was Flash. While it started life as a drawing tool (first released as SmartSketch by FutureWare), it soon became the tool of choice for web developers who wanted to create more interactive pages because of the resulting documents' small file sizes, owing largely to the use of vector graphics. Flash grew to include a timeline for animation and scripting capabilities (ActionScript), and soon, Flash plug-ins were developed for all browsers so they could support Flash pages.

Macromedia also released Fireworks (a tool for creating web graphics), Director (a program that used a timeline and programming language to assist designers in creating interactive content for the Web, desktop and CD-ROMs) and a host of other packages.

In 2005, Macromedia was bought out by Adobe, and it became part of their suite of design tools.

Adobe was founded in 1982 and is still perhaps best known for Photoshop, a photo-editing software suite that became one of the graphic design staples. Its popularity is such that any photo-editing is now referred to as being 'photoshopped'. Photoshop is a bitmap editor, and this means it works with images composed of pixels, though it does have some vector-based capabilities.

Pixels are individual coloured squares that make up an image. Much like a pointillist painting (made up of dots), the viewer will not see the pixels unless they zoom in – the pixels are so small that they blend when viewed at normal scale.

Illustrator was first released in 1987, and unlike Photoshop, this program works with vectors rather than pixels. Vector file sizes tend to be a lot smaller than pixel-based files, as much less information is stored. Vector graphics are made up of points positioned on the x and y axes of the artboard, and the path that links the points. The style of the path is recorded, and this is referred to as the stroke. The path can also be filled by a colour, and thus, give the appearance of a shape. The resulting paths can be simple or complex, but the information stored in the file will always be less than a bitmap graphic. This means that Illustrator is great for flat graphics and logotypes, as the paths can be scaled and will never lose quality (a bitmap will pixelate if the size of the image is increased).

Adobe also developed InDesign, an application similar to QuarkXPress, however, as this application was designed to work seamlessly with the rest of the Adobe offer, it soon became the tool of choice for many digital designers.

In addition to the range of packages for creating print, interactive and web content, there are also numerous products that allow designers to manipulate and edit video and sound. QuickTime was developed by Apple, and is now one of the most used platforms for displaying video, sound and interactive content on the Web, via drives and straight from the desktop.

In terms of editing video, Premiere and After Effects are Adobe packages that allow the user to import, edit and manipulate video and sound recordings. Apple also have specialist tools for editing such as Final Cut and Logic, but importantly, they also provide free, entry level packages such as GarageBand, and iMovie. While these are more basic, they share similar interfaces and functions to their specialist counterparts, and thus make it easier for users to work up to the full systems.

More recent innovations have come in the forms of 3D software such as Maya, Blender and SketchUp, the rise of affordable 3D printers for creating physical artefacts, and the increase in devices that allow users to enter 3D digital worlds.

A 3D printer in action.
Relatively recent innovations such as the 3D printer will prove significant in the next few years of digital design.

Timeline

Like many innovations, the Internet was born out of a military need. During the Cold War, there were concerns that communications sent via telegram could be too easily intercepted or disrupted, so the idea of the Internet was conceived.

During the 1960s, the US government devised the ARPANET (Advanced Research Projects Agency Network). This system divided information into packets (known as 'packet switching'), and these packets were sent across multiple channels, eventually assembling in the hands of the intended recipient. In 1971, the first email was sent via this network. ARPANET then developed into the Internet, and this system carried a multitude of communications, from hypertext documents to phone calls.

In the 1990s, the first high-speed connections were developed, and around this time, Sir Tim Berners-Lee developed the idea of the World Wide Web – a system for creating, coding and accessing web pages. At this point, he also uploaded the first image to the Internet and set a precedent for much of our modern communication. As the idea behind the Internet was to make content accessible to all, the W3C (www.w3.org) was developed in 1994, and

HTML standards were created to ensure that content was created in a way that is consistent in presentation and formatting.

A variety of browsers were developed to connect users to content on the Internet and to display textual information and images. Netscape Navigator and Internet Explorer were some of the first browsers created. Standards became more and more important, and consistency of presentation was a concern and a challenge for many designers, due to the different rendering engines these browsers employed.

In these early days of the Web, search engines and the idea of indexing was born. The first of these search engines was Archie, which was created in 1990 by Alan Emtage, a student at McGill University in Montreal, Canada. Acting much like a virtual telephone book that searched for content rather than people, these services became vital as the number of sites on the Internet grew so rapidly.

However, 1990, presenting material on the screen was difficult as browser rations were generally 680 pixels wide and 480 pixels high. Additionally, monitors would display only sixteen colours (see below).

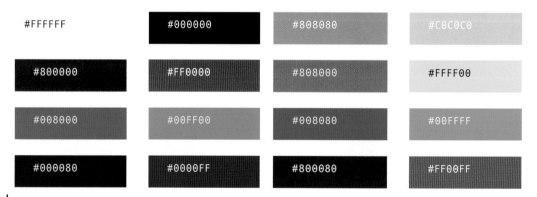

Web-safe colours

The original 16 Web safe colours (converted to CMYK for print). Nowadays, designers can work with the full spectrum of colour. However, in the early days of digital design, entire websites were produced using this limited palette.

16

COMMUNICATION VIA TELEGRAM

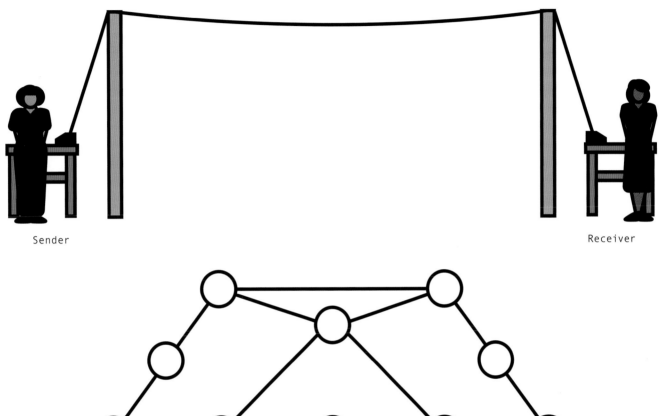

Sender

Receiver

Sender

Receiver

COMMUNICATION VIA THE INTERNET

Communication vis telegram vs. ARPANET's packet switching method.

For many communications, the telegram solution was not secure, and could not transmit large amounts of data. The packet switching method meant that large amounts of information, broken down into smaller chunks, could be ported from sender to receiver. Additionally, the use of multiple channels meant that the information could not be accessed by people listening in.

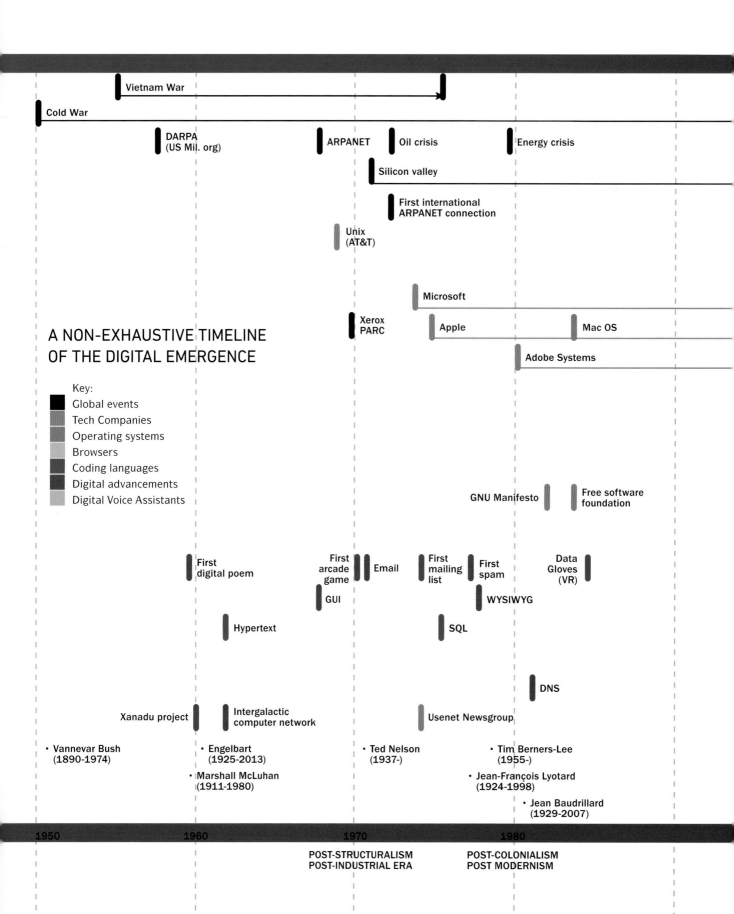

A NON-EXHAUSTIVE TIMELINE
OF THE DIGITAL EMERGENCE

Key:
Global events
Tech Companies
Operating systems
Browsers
Coding languages
Digital advancements
Digital Voice Assistants

Vietnam War

Cold War

DARPA
(US Mil. org)

ARPANET

Oil crisis

Energy crisis

Silicon valley

First international
ARPANET connection

Unix
(AT&T)

Microsoft

Xerox
PARC

Apple

Mac OS

Adobe Systems

GNU Manifesto

Free software
foundation

First
digital poem

First
arcade
game

Email

First
mailing
list

First
spam

Data
Gloves
(VR)

GUI

WYSIWYG

Hypertext

SQL

DNS

Xanadu project

Intergalactic
computer network

Usenet Newsgroup

• Vannevar Bush
(1890-1974)

• Engelbart
(1925-2013)

• Ted Nelson
(1937-)

• Tim Berners-Lee
(1955-)

• Marshall McLuhan
(1911-1980)

• Jean-François Lyotard
(1924-1998)

• Jean Baudrillard
(1929-2007)

1950

1960

1970

1980

POST-STRUCTURALISM
POST-INDUSTRIAL ERA

POST-COLONIALISM
POST MODERNISM

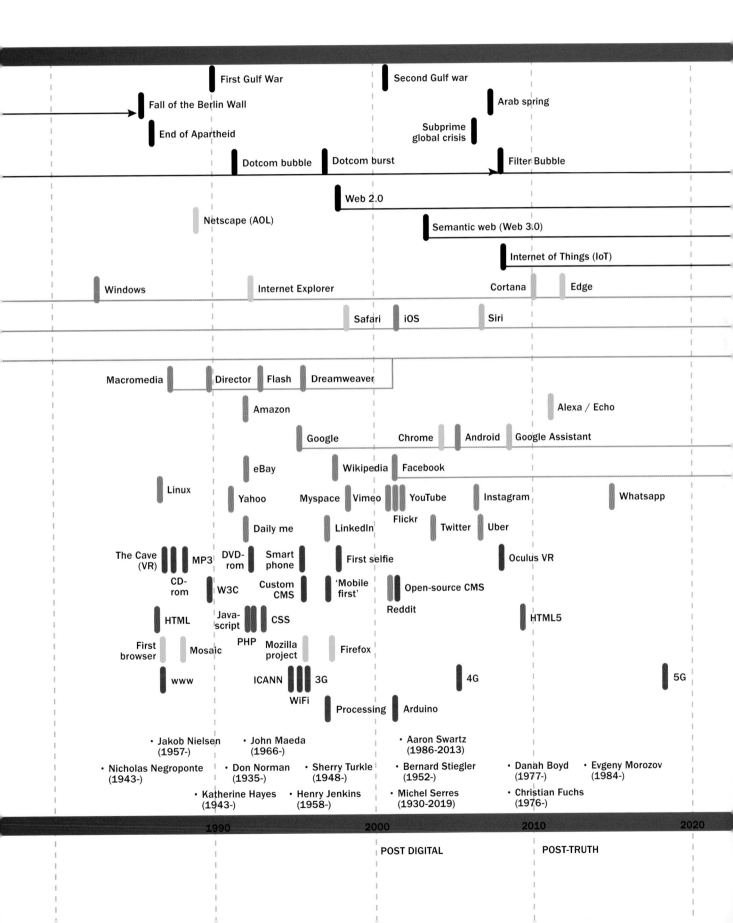

First Gulf War

Second Gulf war

Fall of the Berlin Wall

Arab spring

End of Apartheid

Subprime global crisis

Dotcom bubble   Dotcom burst

Filter Bubble

Web 2.0

Netscape (AOL)

Semantic web (Web 3.0)

Internet of Things (IoT)

Windows

Internet Explorer

Cortana   Edge

Safari   iOS   Siri

Macromedia   Director   Flash   Dreamweaver

Amazon

Alexa / Echo

Google   Chrome   Android   Google Assistant

eBay   Wikipedia   Facebook

Linux

Yahoo   Myspace   Vimeo   YouTube   Instagram   Whatsapp

Flickr

Daily me   LinkedIn   Twitter   Uber

The Cave (VR)   MP3   DVD-rom   Smart phone   First selfie   Oculus VR

CD-rom   W3C   Custom CMS   'Mobile first'   Open-source CMS

Reddit

HTML   Java-script   CSS   HTML5

First browser   Mosaic   PHP   Mozilla project   Firefox

www   ICANN   3G   4G   5G

WiFi

Processing   Arduino

· Jakob Nielsen (1957-)

· John Maeda (1966-)

· Aaron Swartz (1986-2013)

· Nicholas Negroponte (1943-)

· Don Norman (1935-)

· Sherry Turkle (1948-)

· Bernard Stiegler (1952-)

· Danah Boyd (1977-)

· Evgeny Morozov (1984-)

· Katherine Hayes (1943-)

· Henry Jenkins (1958-)

· Michel Serres (1930-2019)

· Christian Fuchs (1976-)

1990   2000   2010   2020

POST DIGITAL   POST-TRUTH

The intention of the Internet

Visionaries and pioneers

As shown in the previous section, there is no one unique inventor of the Web, but a series of technological advances developed by a number of researchers, scientists and engineers. There are as many needs and motivations as there were visionary contributors, and many of these pioneers worked independently from the governmental framework and had very different motivations.

We can differentiate some branches such as humanist, encyclopedist and, later, utopists. People like Tim Berners-Lee were driven by humanist momentum based on the model of the Renaissance Republic of Letters, which fostered the sharing of knowledge and resources to make research more efficient.

Others, such as Vannevar Bush and Ted Nelson were interested in externalising and expanding natural human memory and developed indexation abilities. Their wish was for all people to have information 'at fingers reach' while making all available media (microfilms, photographs, etc.) convergent.

Stewart Brand, a pioneer in community building, developed a new kind of community in order to sustain an alternate power. This work laid the groundwork for a certain level of political emancipation. This alternative community was developed through the use of technology. By making this technology open source, it was then available to a great number of people, in turn facilitating social change with greater ease and connectedness. [See also: Digital utopia, techno-utopianism, page 206]

The groups that developed were numerous, and they had a range of objectives – one group promoted an agora (an open, public space to debate), another promoted a free, ubiquitous universal library, while another promoted an anti-authoritarianism system (a system where authority is shared between its members instead of being centralised and monopolised by an elite).

In the early 90s, if you had to access to a computer (this was likely in a governmental or educational context, but otherwise, the price of a personal computer was still prohibitive), the Internet's content was free of charge and independent; it was a place to entertain, to share, to discuss ideas. It was about being a citizen of the world, or at least it appeared this way. As the Internet grew, political and economic powers began to take note, and things began to change.

What is your business model?

If you look at the history of the Internet as early as 1983, you will find the first attempts at enabling users to shop from home, or as it would later be labelled, e-commerce. However, in the 80s the Internet was still tightly controlled and quite simply, the interest and technology wasn't there.

In 1991, the NSF (National Science Foundation, a US governmental organisation) lifted some of the commercial restrictions on the Web when ANS, a US based non-profit organisation, was granted, under specific conditions, the use of the NSF infrastructure network. The conditions, widely debated on forums at the time, included fees for users who did not belong to any governmental or educational institution.

In 1993, there were 7,500 registered domain names and more than 2 million connected computers. The first ever ad banner (a landscape image to be clicked) was created for AT&T and displayed on the *Wired* website. In 1995, there were 12,000 registered domain names and 16 million users. (Source: http://www. Internetworldstats.com/emarketing.htm).

Also in 1993 Ebay.com was launched. While it was initially intended as a personal page, it has since become one of the largest e-commerce websites. A victim of its own success, eBay had to find a business model in order to survive: the larger its audience grew, the more bandwidth was required, and this lead to an increase of the website hosting costs. This rapid expansion drove the owner to create a business model to sustain the costs of its website (domain name, server space, server maintenance, website maintenance, moderation, research and development, etc.) and the website became a massive success.

By 1995, the Internet had moved forwards rapidly, yet monitors could still only display 256 colours on an 800x600 square pixel surface. Designers were restricted to 'Web safe fonts' include font-folder staples such as Times New Roman and Courier New. 1995 also marks the advent of targeted ad placement, the point at which marketing strategies started to impact the layout of web pages.

1997 marks the first appearance of pop-ups, those small, inopportune browser windows that used to open behind the main page to promote a service or a product. This intrusive marketing strategy quickly proved to be counter-productive as it irked Internet users.

In 1998, monitors grew and could now display a 1024x768 square pixel design, this gave web designers a larger canvas to play with. The rise of Flash interactive animations (launched in 1996) meant more designers without coding backgrounds could satisfy the increasing need for multimodal/multimedia content, easily creating pages that incorporated sound, animation, video, games and more. Following the path of Net Art, although with different motivations, emerged Flash Art. [See also: Art on / with the Internet, page 172]

1998 also marks the privatisation of the Internet. With more than 2 million domain names and more than 100 million, the NSF took a step back in favour of the ICANN (Internet Corporation for Assigned Numbers and Names, a US non-profit organisation) for the registration of domain names.

Developments

The dotcom bubble

Dotcoms are the name given to mid-90s companies that bet on telecommunication and new technologies as a means of increasing their financial growth. Despite the common belief that companies without significant physical assets, such as shopfronts, are cheaper to run than traditional ones, they still require substantial long-term investment. A large amount of funding is required to develop the company's infrastructure and ensure sustainability and growth – as the company grows, it needs effective design, marketing and development of technical aspects.

Fuelled by the success story of some Silicon Valley entrepreneurs (circa the year 2000), venture capitalists, investors and traders overestimated the values of some young companies that were far from generating profit. It lead to an over-speculation on empty shells when pitches were based more on dreams than on functional products (much of this excitement was based on little more than unchecked statistics and PowerPoint presentations without any reasonable business model, rather than carefully mapped research and development). Optimism fuelled by new technology turned into euphoria, and stocks soared.

Between 1999 and 2001, the dotcom bubble burst and many workers of the Web economy lost their jobs as companies were forced to close. From the crash, only a few companies survived, and some of them are still part of our daily Internet landscape (Amazon, eBay). However, it took almost a decade for the Web economy to retrieve economic credibility and the trust of significant investors.

Participative spaces

Far from the tumult of the Web economy, and applying the Free Foundation Software precept, in 2001, Jimmy Wales and Larry Sanger founded Wikipedia. This platform is an ad-free content encyclopedia, running on a wiki engine, under the GNU (a free Unix-like operating system) Free Documentation License.

The content of Wikipedia is managed by its community, and this is not without controversy. Relying on the goodwill of anonymous and unpaid experts in their field for the sharing of knowledge was, in the early 2000s, not an obvious step forward for a society whose intellectual elites generated information and ideas that were centralised and shrouded in a heavy, often impenetrable, hierarchy.

The success of Wikipedia is quantifiable by its popularity. It proves that a simple interface is enough to attract people, as long as the usability and the content of the website are of quality. Because Wikipedia is run as a non-profit organisation, it also shows us that the sharing economy and society of participation is sustainable. Finally, it clearly demonstrates that people are ready to work together and share information en masse for the wider benefit of society.

Even today, Wikipedia has not lost its place among the ranks of the top academic referencing systems; it is recognised as a useful and sustainable source for general knowledge, updated in near real-time.

Web 2.0

A popular term since 2003–2004, Web 2.0 marks both the introduction of mass user-centred functionality within the Web, and the advent of new marketing strategies to give the net economy a new lease of life after the burst of the dotcom bubble.

In 2003-2004, there were 800 million regular Internet users in the world (about 13 per cent of the population), and monitors could display more than sixteen million colours [see Chapter 4, Designing for the Web and platforms: Colour for the Web], but smartphones did not yet offer a web-like experience.

The Web 2.0 technology offered a huge boost to small businesses that wanted to create, modify and update the content of their website, without having to hire an external service provider or learn markup and programming language. Content Management Systems (CMS), such as Drupal (2000), WordPress (2003), and Joomla! (2005), offered this functionality and furthermore, were highly accessible as they were (and still are) largely supported by the open-source community and therefore were free (apart from hosting and domain name costs). [See also: Content management systems, page 152]

The Web 2.0 functionality also facilitated the emergence of blogs (an individual online journal), and these quickly flourished. The year 1999 saw the creation of the Blogger platform, and in that year, less than twenty-five blogs were created. The number of blogs increased to a figure in excess of fifty million in 2006, a year that saw the introduction of functionality such as permalinks, blogrolls and trackbacks. The developments unveiled in 2006 fostered a greater feeling of belonging in virtual spaces as users created communities based on interests and made virtual friends across the globe. These friendship groups spread across social media platforms and have lead to a massive amount of user-created content (democratisation of means of production), supported by advanced usability (it is easy to share content) and interoperability (it is easy to access content from any kind of device).

The growing usage of smartphones, boosted by the emergence of touchscreen devices (largely heralded by the introduction of the iPhone in 2007), greatly assisted the stratospheric rise and development of social media. These devices have also impacted on web design, leading to the use of grids to facilitate responsivity [See also: Chapter 5: Web 2.0: Layouts for the Web] and touchscreen devices have also expanded the field of interface design and the whole design workflow [See also: Chapter 7: The roles].

The extensive use of nomad devices such as smartphones, tablets and laptops, combined with high capacity networks, brought about the increased use of cloud computing and storing. These cloud services are accessible from any digital device through dedicated applications that are used to document our daily life (photographs for example), but services such as Github and Dropbox use similar technologies to share work resources between co-workers, irrespective of geography.

2010 onwards

With more devices available to be connected to the Internet, and with more tools to create and share content, the way we used to choose, buy and experience cultural goods evolved significantly. Dematerialisation of content led to an exponential growth in the consumption of music (streaming services, music e-stores), movies (Torrent sites, YouTube, Netflix, etc.) and books. Whether these materials were obtained legally or not, the change in the way the media is consumed by many has transformed the landscape of the cultural and media industries. Material artefacts are still created and sold, though one might argue these are seen by the masses as archaic. However, the need for many to recapture the essential aura of physical materials (vinyl records, hard copy books, the experience of sitting in a cinema) that cannot be replicated digitally has led people to invest more in items perceived to be culturally significant and of high value, much to the delight of paper-based designers.

Since 2017, most shopping is done online, and under the cover of marketing optimisation, persuasive design is used and perhaps overused; the journey of users is monitored, their data stored and analysed, and their behaviour profiled. Even on social media, anonymity and privacy may no longer be granted. [See also: Social media, page 162]

Beyond the questions related to the ownership of user-generated content (artwork but also comments and ratings), behaviour data and profiles are sold, unknown to the Web user. [See also: Dark UX / UI: Ethics and design for bad, page 208]

Additionally, in the name of customisation of services/individualisation of content, websites tend, through algorithms, to filter data and display only information that users would likely react positively to (recommended purchases and news feed), exposing them only to what they are keen to read, hear and watch, confining them to a kind of cultural bubble disconnected to the complexity of real social powers.

```
1  <!DOCTYPE html>
2  <html>
3     <head>
4        <title>lipsum</title>
5     </head>
6     <body>
7  <p>Lorem ipsum dolor sit amet, consectetur adipiscing elit. Vestibulum consectetur turpis nibh, nec tincidunt metus maximus sit amet.
   Donec et aliquam odio. Duis eget congue ligula. In accumsan ligula in tortor imperdiet tempus. Maecenas dui neque, dictum in ultricies
   ac, aliquet quis erat. Aliquam faucibus, quam malesuada rhoncus convallis, ligula mi blandit elit, ac eleifend nisl urna ac leo. Morbi
   vel augue vitae odio consectetur ornare. Donec non ligula eu sem lacinia suscipit pharetra id odio. Integer in tortor eu augue lacinia
   semper non sit amet libero. Quisque elementum, nisi rhoncus pretium suscipit, est nibh congue elit, sit amet rhoncus ex elit in nibh. Sed
   urna risus, congue sit amet libero nec, lacinia viverra ante. Mauris sapien magna, interdum ut velit et, cursus semper felis.
8  </p>
9  <p>In malesuada ipsum purus, quis tincidunt velit facilisis eget. Etiam volutpat fermentum diam eu tristique. Nunc tincidunt sed lectus
   eget accumsan. Suspendisse interdum luctus velit volutpat scelerisque. Pellentesque lobortis augue dui, sed cursus tellus elementum
   iaculis. Pellentesque habitant morbi tristique senectus et netus et malesuada fames ac turpis egestas. Duis volutpat commodo egestas.
   Donec sagittis magna ut ante viverra, eget consequat ligula laoreet. Cras felis augue, fermentum in varius ultrices, sollicitudin a
   nulla. Donec porttitor magna eu tellus rhoncus, vitae hendrerit ante efficitur. Etiam molestie hendrerit quam, id efficitur ligula
   eleifend sed. Nam convallis fermentum orci, et tincidunt ex bibendum et.
10 </p>
11 <p>Morbi elementum sapien eget ultricies bibendum. Nunc eget elit in purus ultrices bibendum. Curabitur faucibus, dui at suscipit
   pulvinar, arcu nisi cursus massa, vitae molestie augue diam a elit. Proin ac nulla neque. Ut cursus erat turpis. Aenean in viverra magna.
   Nam in ante viverra, eleifend metus quis, pellentesque leo. Nullam ultrices dolor in est congue, non finibus odio dictum. Fusce risus
   est, luctus finibus urna eu, tempor venenatis erat. Etiam porttitor orci sed tempor porttitor.
12 </p>
13 <p>Pellentesque maximus suscipit risus sit amet auctor. Curabitur congue nisl nisi, eu tempus sapien efficitur et. In pharetra tristique
   dui, at vehicula mauris sodales ut. Quisque ullamcorper, nisl eget cursus mollis, urna diam accumsan tellus, a suscipit massa nisi ut
   augue. Etiam euismod iaculis ligula sed faucibus. Suspendisse tempor est at fermentum molestie. Class aptent taciti sociosqu ad litora
   torquent per conubia nostra, per inceptos himenaeos. Aenean in mi eget arcu lobortis consequat quis non ipsum. Suspendisse eu lectus
   sagittis, imperdiet magna vitae, tempor tellus. Pellentesque auctor dolor quam, vel faucibus sapien sodales cursus. In porttitor nunc a
   velit feugiat, a tincidunt urna luctus. Maecenas fringilla eleifend lorem et porttitor.
14 </p>
15 <p>Pellentesque erat elit, facilisis faucibus euismod at, euismod nec metus. Duis elit tortor, lacinia id posuere nec, efficitur et dui.
   Ut ut mollis sem. Nunc quis leo quam. Nullam scelerisque dapibus arcu in consectetur. Pellentesque non ullamcorper mauris, elementum
   ultricies urna. Sed consectetur eget arcu vitae aliquet. Phasellus sit amet tortor ut erat dictum cursus at facilisis dolor. Proin
   ullamcorper, metus non faucibus iaculis, dolor mauris lobortis dolor, et vulputate massa ipsum maximus augue.
16 </p>
17    </body>
18 </html>
19
```

Hypertext Mark-up Language (HTML)

This mark-up language revolutionised the way we display data on a screen as it afforded designers possibilities similar to those achieved with print design: columns, visual hierarchies, typeface choices, and options for styling text.

The principles of Web design

The main intent of the Internet is to communicate information, and design should not impede or distract from this. Sites should be effective and easy to use by all, regardless of ability and experience.

Accessibility

Accessibility has always been a primary concern for web designers, and to ensure all designers have a benchmark to work to, the W3C has laid out very clear standards that should be met. One of the main themes is the correct use of semantic code – this means the correct use of HTML elements, and employing CSS to style these. As an example, one should use the `<strong> </strong>` tags to make a word bold and then style it rather than writing a unique CSS class [more on this in Chapter 3: Coding and markup languages]. The reason for this parity of practice is that site readers will emphasise any work surrounded by the strong tags, but they will not be able to interpret non-uniform selectors that individual designers have created.

A designer should always keep presentation (skin) and content (bones) separate. Elements can be styled using HTML, but they should not be – presentation should always be affected by CSS, as this means consistent rules are applied across the multiple pages of a site, and changes are quicker to implement (if you change one rule in CSS, the entire site will see this change and interpret it in the same way).

Again, layouts should be devised and implemented with CSS, not HTML. During the dark ages of website design, when CSS was in its infancy, many designers used tables and framesets to control layouts, but these were not created for styling purposes, and for that reason, they were difficult to control. Firstly, CSS allows for more styling options that work effectively across browsers, and perhaps more importantly

to modern web designers, it also allows for variations in layouts should a user view the site on a mobile device or tablet.

Form (ever) follows function?

Formulated as a reaction against the excess of ornamentation seen in applied arts at the beginning of the twentieth century, the phrase 'form ever follows function' encapsulated the modernist architectural approach: the final shape of an artefact is determined by its function(s).

The phrase implies that design is not simply a varnish applied at the last instance to make the artefact look pretty, but rather that designers should be involved from the conception of a project, alongside engineers and builders, from the outset, to ensure the artefact developed offers both the right aesthetic and functional experience. The beauty of a product stems from the facility of its usage, and it is the fruit of well-balanced forces.

Applying this idea to the development of new technologies, this motto may sound deceiving at first. Since most of the functionality of a new digital product will be unfamiliar to the public, and sometimes even blended and hidden, this could be perplexing and confusing for the end-user. The unfamiliarity will likely trigger the questions such as 'What is it for?' and 'How does it work?'. For example, think about the first time you held a smartphone – consider how the design of the artefact helped you understand how it should be used.

You know how to switch on the light by pushing a button on the wall, because the reaction, the visual and tactile feedback, are immediate and therefore, clearly correlated. The shape of the artefact implies the correct use (this is called 'affordance') and the learning process is quick, almost playful. However, how do you know how to access the information on a website as there are no physical buttons, or paper pages to turn? Even the shape of the website might take an unexpected form, such as a full-screen video that autoplays, an interactive diagram, animated gifs, or a parallax scrolling functionality. In this instance of designing for online environments, there is a physical disconnect – although you may click and move a mouse, the outcome is a movement of pixels that simulate an event in real life.

The 'form' of a website should reveal as much about its function as a book, a door handle or a kettle. This is accessible interface design.

For around the first decade of web design, a mimicry of old media was used to explain functionality. The success of the Apple desktop model led to the extensive and sometimes exaggerated use of visual metaphors – the background of the page should look like the material of a wooden office desk, a button should appear in relief with dropped shadow and click when it is pressed. These metaphors did not tell the user anything about the content of the information contained in the application or website, but it gave the methods of navigation and surface design a recognisable feel. This approach of employing visual metaphor to explain new concepts is called, in the realm of design, 'skeuomorphism' or 'skeuomorphic style'.

Skeuomorphism was not always of a good taste, but it gave a reassuring landmark to end-users. The flat interface of the screen functioned as a reduced version of the physical world, a place all users instinctively knew how to interact with. However, more functionality was developed that had no equivalent in the real world, so it became difficult to reference the existing physical things, therefore, the Web interface needed to disconnect from literal visual translations and develop its

own visual code. Over time, the public got used to the Web's structure and gestural grammar, such as clicking a hypertext link or tab, pop-ups, forms, rollover and rollouts, variations of scrolling functionality, etc., so designers now can create pieces that rely less on visual metaphor and instead utilise this new visual language.

After skeuomorphism came the 'flat design' style – this was far less referential, maybe even less narrative, and this also has its pitfalls. With its use of sans serif, modernist influenced typography and tiled/blocky layouts, flat design quickly became all-pervasive due to its use by leading tech companies. However, its flatness became off-putting to many who wanted more of a human touch and a design with a bit of individual personality.

Within the modern context of web design, juggling the constraints of responsivity and the interoperability you will have to address when constructing an online environment, plus the level of digital literacy of your target audience, you should ask yourself: What is more important, the information presented on a website, the presentation of that information, or the way it is accessed?

The answer to a degree is all three of the above – users will not trust a site that is badly designed (that is to say, a site where the information is not quickly accessible), but no amount of polish can cover-up, or enhance, substandard content or a poor navigation system.

[See also: Chapter 4: Designing for the Web and platforms, and What is Technological determinism?, page 202.]

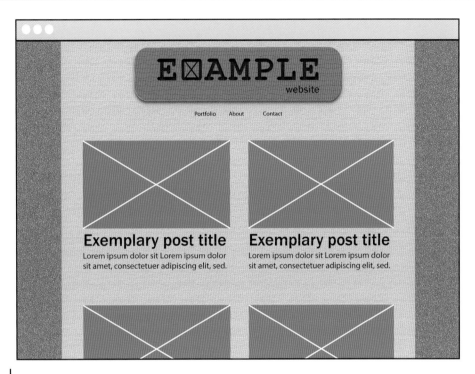

Skeuomorphism and flat design

The skeuomorphic design above incorporates elements of texture to make the page look more 'real'; the design below eschews skeuomorphic traditions as contemporary web users are more sophisticated and the design does not need to reference other 'real-life' things to be understood.

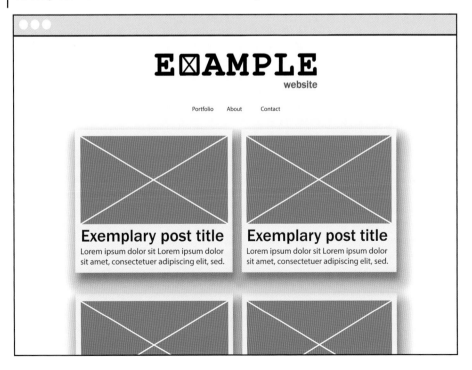

Semiotics

Semiotics is the study of signs and symbols and how these indicate specific meaning to specific groups of people. It addresses the arbitrary link between any given sign and the meaning that is attached to it. This means there is no natural or in-built link or connection, and the sign and its intended meaning has to be learnt.

For example, a hamburger menu (the sign) on a website signals to a viewer that they have to click to see the levels of navigation (what is signified, or meant by the symbol). However, there is no inherent link between the symbol and menu systems, it has to be learnt. Once these symbols reach enough people, the meaning becomes common wisdom.

The sign may also hold different meanings depending on who is viewing it, and colour is the best example of this. In the west, the colour red can signal passion, anger and danger, however, in the far east, the colour often symbolises luck.

Moving back to web design, you might also use the terms 'denotation' and 'connotation' to describe how viewers access and understand information. As digital technologies are still relatively new, they have adopted some conventions from print, but there are some unique elements that cannot be described by common equivalents, so a new language had to be developed.

When the Web was very new, hypertext links were very confusing for many everyday users. People were used to reading text, but had no history of clicking on words in order to go to another page. However, they were used to clicking buttons on a remote control. To make it more obvious that a certain thing needed to be clicked, designers began to make the links look more like a realistic button, often adding shading and texture. To use the aforementioned terms, a button was denoted, and the connotations of this were 'click and an action will happen,' much like your remote control at home.

Even on a single website, you will use CSS to create and follow conventions that will enable the viewer to navigate your pages with ease. You will use hierarchies to signal which content is most important (normally a larger font, perhaps at a different weight, in a unique colour), and once this convention is established, you should follow it on future pages.

Icon	The sign	Signifies (what the sign means)
≡	Hamburger menu symbol	Click for links
✉	Envelope	Click to send someone an email
⌂	Icon of a house	Click to go back to the home page

The semiotics of web icons

The icons above will no doubt feel familiar to you. However, the meaning behind these symbols is not inherent in the graphic itself; it is learnt, and it is only through good design that their function is made apparent to users that have not previously encountered them.

The Internet

The Internet

The Internet

The Internet

The Internet

The Internet

The semiotics of web typography

Which of the above typefaces look 'correct' to you?

Do any of the above typeface choices look 'wrong'?

Think about the associations you have with each typeface and consider what has affected this. The Internet is an idea that embodies specific associations and therefore, as designers, we may feel the need to present it in a certain way, using assets that convey this meaning.

Gestalt

Gestalt theory comes from the psychology field; it is an early twentieth-century theoretical framework that describes the way we perceive visual information (the figures) and how our mind processes/organises visual data. Its principle is commonly summarised as: 'The whole is different from the sum of its parts.' The laws of Gestalt could also be combined to reinforce a set of information and make the navigation easy.

Applied to web design, Gestalt framework implies that every individual and beautifully crafted element, button, menu, head, white space, should be put together carefully, to not only keep their own aesthetic and functional qualities, but also to make sense within the web page. Since Gestalt is as much about aesthetics as functionality, it should be taken into consideration at the early stage of the design process.

Emergence

The whole is identified before the parts: a person will look at your designs as a (pleasing) whole before they start to seek hierarchies and structures. At first sight, users should identify whether they are in the place they were looking for, whether they will find information quickly or, conversely, if it is a place to wander.

The example website shown below gives users a clear idea of emergence. At first, you will see a page, then, very quickly, you will identify the elements that make up the page.

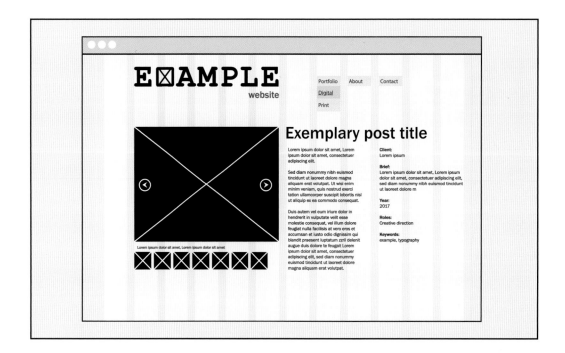

Simplicity

People do not invest the same amount of time in accessing a web page as they would a book. An audience wants to access information quickly and with relatively little fuss. One commonly used term to describe this is KISS, or *keep it simple, stupid*. Even a great narrative can be told with fewer visual elements than you think; sometimes, white/empty spaces are more powerful than an image or colour-saturated page, like the design opposite.

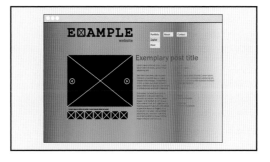

Figure and ground

In editorial design, the foreground bears the data that users look for. You do not need to use a tiled animated gif in the background, even if technically it is easy to do: yes, it will catch the attention of users, but for how long? If they cannot properly focus on the content of your website, they won't stay long, and they won't come back. Elements that carry meaning (text, navigation bar, etc.) should be clearly separated from the background to avoid the user's eyes jumping from one area to another.

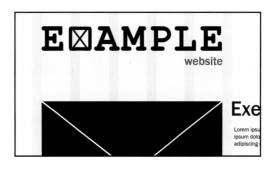

Symmetry and order (harmony)

Our brain is constantly looking for patterns. A good website will have a clear layout that will help users to predict the position of visual information (where to find what) and anticipate micro or macro actions (scroll, click, etc.). Symmetry is a good way to bring order to a range of content that has varying degrees of importance. Breaking the symmetry or creating an anomaly will create an impression of imbalance, which will lead the eyes to the component that designers have highlighted, such as a pull quote, subheading, or an important link. To facilitate variation with symmetry and anomalies, designers use a system of grids, the most common one being a twelve-column grid, as seen opposite. [For more, see page 150.]

Proximity (also called 'grouping')

Items in close proximity are perceived as being part of the same group — think letters in a word. White space, such as a gutter between two columns or between two paragraphs of text, can be used to divide groups. Two columns of text will be perceived as part of a group if the space between the columns is smaller than the space around the whole article.

Exemplary post title

Lorem ipsum dolor sit amet, Lorem ipsum dolor sit amet, consectetuer adipiscing elit.

Sed diam nonummy nibh euismod tincidunt ut laoreet dolore magna aliquam erat volutpat. Ut wisi enim minim veniam, quis nostrud exerci tation ullamcorper suscipit lobortis nisl ut aliquip ex ea commodo consequat.

Duis autem vel eum iriure dolor in hendrerit in vulputate velit esse molestie consequat, vel illum dolore

Client:
Lorem ipsum

Brief:
Lorem ipsum dolor sit amet, Lorem ipsum dolor sit amet, consectetuer adipiscing elit, sed diam nonummy nibh euismod tincidunt ut laoreet dolore m

Year:
2017

Roles:
Creative direction

Similarity (also known as 'invariance')

When we see items that are similar in appearance, we tend to group them and thus infer they have the same usage, action and semantic value. Designing similar-looking objects on a web page creates connections; you can achieve this by using the same colour, size, shape or typographic choices. Similarities will help the end-user to find their path through your website, so make all links look the same, limit your typographic palette and be consistent with the way you create icons — create a simple system and follow this.

Portfolio   About   Contact

Digital

Print

Exemplary post title

Lorem ipsum dolor sit amet, Lorem ipsum dolor sit amet, consectetuer adipiscing elit.

Client:
Lorem ipsum

Dominance

In order to achieve a hierarchy, one element needs to have dominance. Headlines, for example, cannot be too similar to the body copy – they need to stand out. However, a headline should not look completely at odds with the rest of the design. This can be achieved by creating a contrast in scale, weight or colour, but don't employ too many marks of difference or else elements will stand out for the wrong reasons.

Heading 1
Heading 2
HEADING 3

Lorem ipsum dolor sit amet, consectetuer adipiscing elit, sed diam nonummy nibh euismod tincidunt ut laoreet dolore m

Continuity and expectations

Our eyes tend to follow a path, a direction indicated by visual elements on a page. The eye will continue the dynamic initiated by your layout, and you can use this to invite the user to scroll. Add a clue at the bottom of your page to tell the user that there is more content to follow, such as a typographic arrangement that suggests there is more.

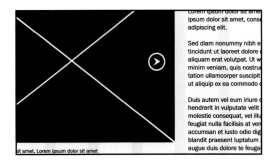

Past experience

Users want to access information quickly, so make it easy.

Be creative, but use some simple conventions that the user will quickly identify and trust. As we discussed in the semiotics section, a hamburger menu is a well-known convention that signals to a majority of people that a menu will drop down if they click on it.

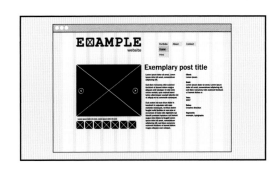

Additionally, the structure of a page can be created to reference a user's typical experience of the Web: contact information and quick links tend to go in the footer whereas the search tool is normally located on the top right of the page.

Keep navigation, logos, etc., in the same place on each page and, if you have some pioneer spirit, introduce only one innovative feature (functionality, navigation path, etc.) on your new website to give people time to get used to it —make it easy for the viewer.

The browser

The browser is the tool that houses your beautiful designs and presents them to the audience. Essentially, it is just a tool to read and render your mark-up language and code. In the background, it downloads your assets (text, image, video, audio, etc.) and then presents them in the manner you intended with CSS.

One issue all web designers face is that while the browser displays HTML (using a rendering engine), despite W3C recommendations, each browser has its own rules, and all browsers have some unique quirks. These quirks all mean the designer has to occasionally learn workarounds to ensure parity of viewing experience. While things are much improved and there is less difference in rendering between say, Google Chrome and Safari, new browsers are always being developed, and older ones are always being updated – any of these innovations can bring about new problems for the designer as much as they may offer opportunities.

The web browser market share as of 2017, was split between these different companies:

- Chrome (Google/Alphabet, first released in 2008): 59 per cent

- Safari (Apple, first released in 2003): 15 per cent web browser market share

- Internet Explorer (Microsoft, released 1995, and no longer supported from 2018) + Microsoft Edge (Microsoft, first released in 2015): 9 per cent

- Firefox (Mozilla Foundation, first released in 2002): 7 per cent

- Opera (first released in 1996): 4 per cent

- Tor (The Onion Router), for an anonymity network journey.

- When designing a web page, do not hesitate to check how its elements are supported in different browsers and on a range of devices (computer, tablet and mobile).

The Internet Explorer web browser
Through the late 1990s, this was perhaps the most common portal to the world wide web.

Hyperlinks and non-linear content

Hyperlinks are one of the main components of the Web. The concept of associating text with additional content and references is not new and is deeply rooted in the literary tradition. From manuscripts with marginalia to academic footnotes, literature has always employed cross-referencing, commenting and additional text, which adds its own perspective to a source document.

What makes the hyperlink so special is its malleability. Hyperlinks are easy to implement into an HTML page, and these can be applied to text and images. These links can lead to new information, pages, or media (.PDF, .Zip, etc.), and they are part of a never-ending associative network. Unlike most books, a page using hyperlinks offers a non-linear reading or navigation – its content is then said to be disruptive.

There are several types of links on the Web:

- links that call up a new page in the same window or in a new tab

- links connected to an internal or external anchor, that is to say, to a specific section of a page

- MailTo: links that open the email client of the user and pre-fill some information, such as the email address

- links to an alternate way of displaying the page (increasing the body text point size for accessibility, for example)

- lastly, there are links that send a request to a database (search button, tags, next/previous page, etc.).

Since the Web's infancy, hyperlinks have been coloured electric blue if the associated links have not already been visited. If a browser has a record of the page being visited, the links will appear purple. Usage and display of links have evolved and, nowadays, the design of each hyperlink depends mainly on the web page information hierarchy and its style, as defined by the CSS file. [For more see: CSS, page 90.]

Typically a simple HTML hyperlink looks like this:

```
<a href="http://www.example.com">My
clickable text leading to my example
website</a>
```

The target URL is defined on the left, the clickage text on the right.

Types of hyperlinks and types of links, their attributes and their design will be detailed further in Chapter 3: Coding and markup languages.

Hyperlinks

This image illustrates the non-linear reading possibilities afforded by the Web. Unlike a book, which is typically read from front to back, any webpage can link to another within the same website, or hyperlinks can take users to other pages from across the Web, bringing together communities, content, and ideas.

Types of websites (topology of the Web)

There are many types of websites, and as the needs of users expand, so do the opportunities and possibilities of web builds. From online shops to databases, and portfolio sites to intranets, there are established models that fulfil almost any need.

However, there are many types of sites out there beyond the few searchable websites that you will encounter every day (ones that are indexed and can be found by search engines and are not hidden). In fact, searchable sites account for a very small percentage of all sites.

Below the searchable surface, you have a number of 'hidden' intranets; these are pages that hold company data, human resources information, financial particulars, etc. For very obvious reasons, these sites are not found on Google and can only be accessed by people with the correct credentials.

Beyond this there is the Dark Web. The Dark Web includes many pages that are purposefully hidden from the everyday Internet user, and sometimes it includes content that is purposely hidden from the authorities. This list includes sites that host questionable and illegal content.

Portfolio or shop window

Of the most basic types of websites you may find are portfolios, used to show off the products and services offered, and shop windows that offer information such as an address, contact details and opening hours.

Any type of business, no matter how large or small, will likely have a presence online, and in some cases, this may be no more than a shop window to let the world know they exist. If a website achieves no more than this, you may ask what's the point in having anything at all?

The answer to this is to think about how you look for new places to shop, restaurants to eat in or places to visit. More often than not, people will search for a business online to read reviews, find an address, or simply to check out the services offered. If there is no trace of this business online it can make them look less legitimate or trustworthy.

The idea of the shop window and portfolio sounds simplistic as a notion, but can be vast in its execution and make a noticeable difference to the business. Simply showing up in the right searches can ensure a greater flow of visitors and more trade.

Navigation systems, the right content and metadata are the keys to success. Each image needs alt tags as these are imperative for visually impaired readers; they also help search engines understand what the company offers. Good and useful navigation will again have a positive effect on (SEO), but it will also mean that users are less likely to get confused and go elsewhere. While metadata does not help with rankings in search engines, it does help them categorise the business and place it in the right searches.

Blogs and blogging platforms

After the dotcom bust of 2000, the emergence of platforms such as blogs gave the Internet a much needed new face and approach. Blogging platforms were largely heralded as the beginnings of Web 2.0, as users could now generate content rather than simply accessing it.

These platforms allow everyday people to share their thoughts and opinions online and have them read by an international audience. Groups that share similar interests and ideas can form across continents, and some of these platforms became so popular that a new type of celebrity was formed.

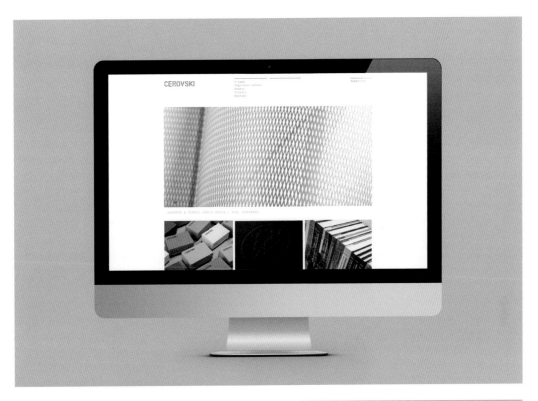

Bunch Design

Cerovski Print Boutique

A 'portfolio' website for Cerovski, a young Croatian print production studio.

Design agency Bunch recently developed a new brand identity for the studio; this included a custom logotype and typeface, website, and a variety of printed collateral.

www.bunchdesign.com

The term 'citizen journalism' was coined to describe a number of bloggers that reported news from the coal face, outside of the constraints of the corporate news world.

Blogs grew to incorporate a variety of approaches when disseminating content. Vlogs (blogs with video-based content) and podcasts (episodic content normally focused on a single subject, presented using audio and/or video) developed as users wanted content that could be consumed on the go, rather than posts they had to sit down and read.

MySpace was one of the early platforms developed that allowed users to interact with people who shared similar tastes. Additionally, MySpace was a platform through which everyday people could create music and share it with an audience on a scale that unsigned artists could not previously reach.

Over time these platforms became more sophisticated and lead to social blogging (Facebook), microblogging (Twitter) and picture blogging (Instagram, Snapchat, Hipstamatic). Each of these platforms has developed in ways that ensured their financial viability by finding ways to use user data to target adverts at the right people. This monetisation of personal data can be viewed as corporate success and neoliberal triumph, but for many users it is also a concern, as to access the platform they have to relinquish rights to their own personal information. Whichever way it is viewed, social blogging is, for many, the main way to stay in touch with friends and family, and for this reason, above all else, it is here to stay.

E-Commerce
The ability for anyone to sell goods online is one of the most levelling and positive effects of the modern Internet. Previously, only companies with vast reach and influence could connect with a global audience, but now anyone with a good product and a website can sell to people on a global scale.

Think about the number of products you have bought online. It's likely you will have purchased some form of entertainment from Amazon, perhaps a handmade artefact direct from the maker, tickets to music or sporting events, subscriptions to magazines, and the list goes on.

In terms of the build of these websites, there are two distinct types of e-commerce platform, one that the company controls directly (Big Cartel and WooCommerce are platforms that support this), and the others are more like middlemen that offer a platform for people to sell online (examples include Etsy and eBay). All of these platforms are made possible by payment platforms like PayPal and Stripe, as these allow users to buy online securely.

As a designer, you will find platforms your client can sell through effortlessly. The best thing is the ease of set-up these platforms offer, and the inbuilt security means you can offer these services to your customers safe in the knowledge that they will be protected.

Wiki
A wiki can be viewed as an online encyclopedia or databank of information that is crowdsourced. This means the facts presented are not compiled by one person, but by a number of experts on the subject. Users may register on sites such as wikipedia.org, and contribute to a page that they have specific insight about. The additions made by these users will often be fact-checked and approved by experts to ensure that facts are correct and nothing misleading or libellous is presented online.

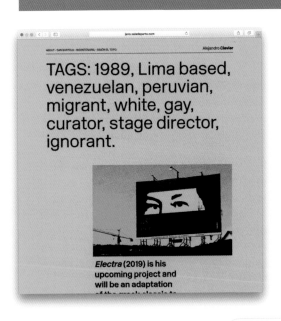

Alexandro Valcarcel

The Revolution Was a Lie

Portfolio website for Alejandro Clavier, a playwright and stage director based in Lima, Peru.

This website design utilises bold, flat, limited colour palette and a simple modernist sans-serif typeface. The treatment of the text is particularly effective - while the font choice is limited, a lot is achieved by introducing a variety of weights and sticking to two colours (white and black).

www.behance.net/avalcarcel

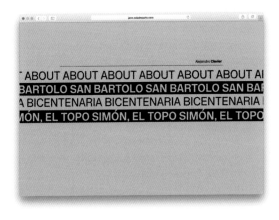

Wikileaks.org is a site used often by whistleblowers to expose alleged wrongdoings by governments, other authorities and big business. Data dumps have become a feature of Wikileaks – whistleblowers have several times uploaded large numbers of files obtained from employers in the hope they will expose some wrongdoing or injustice.

However, wikis may also be far more specific in their objectives and can apply to a single source such as a television programme or one specific artist or designer. These pages are normally set up by fans and they, along with other fans, will compile as much data about the subject as they can, and present it online for others to read.

Public services

Public services websites account for a large proportion of Internet sites. These cover areas of business such as health organisations, tax offices, pensions, museums, universities and more.

Administrative tasks are often consuming: being accessible 24/7, online services should save time and remove stress for the end-user by providing a smooth experience.

Accessibility is especially important when these types of sites are created. While all sites should be fully accessible [see pages 25 and 179 for more detail], it is very likely that a person with a sight impairment or is an elderly person will visit a doctor's website, and anyone can visit the tax office.

In these instances, while the layout and hierarchy of a page is still vital in terms of readability, any superfluous decoration should be avoided as the user needs to access the information they require with little fuss and distraction.

Like online banking, public services address sensitive data: it depends on the designer to provide a safe online experience and to quickly meet the end-user's expectation.

Before designing, it is important to plan the user's journey and to anticipate their needs; leaving them in frustration is the worst-case scenario. UX design will help you to know how the user navigates and uses the website; it will also allow you to determine the habits of users and help you to answer their questions in a minimum number of clicks.

Avoid animated gifs and flickering banners: focus on the hierarchy of information and consistency, and provide users with inclusive tools such as search fields, instructional videos and sitemaps to help them find their way in the way they want.

As the audience of an online service website is very wide, provide options and resources that match user profiles: online forms for well-experienced users, forms to print for less savvy ones.

Do not underestimate the confirmation process: let the user know that their clicks have been validated and their requests registered; there is nothing more upsetting than having to redo a tedious procedure (for example, filling in a twelve-field form) because it wasn't confirmed the first time.

Web portals

Web portals are websites designed to give users access to a dedicated space related to a community, a geographical area, a service or a product. In the 90s, Internet provider web portals were often the default page of the browser.

Web portals bring together resources (links) and services (search engines, mail, news, weather

Pixelfish

a+b furniture

For a+b furniture, Pixelfish designed and constructed a responsive e-commerce site. The design utilises HTML & CSS, with elements of JQuery; it is built on a CMS platform that allows the client to independently make updates and add content without the assistance of a designer or developer.

www.pixelfish.co.uk

forecasting, blogs, forums and entertainment content) from other systems or servers within what are called 'portlets.' Most web portals also propose that their users customise the interface. This requires the interface to be fluid enough to suit the user while keeping the layout consistent and accessible.

For portal users, being able to access a set of services and resources using only one URL is a real asset.

For organisations and businesses, a web portal reinforces their digital presence and creates customer loyalty by providing a consistent look and feel, while increasing their traffic.

Yahoo's portal is one of the most visited commercial ones, but universities and governments have portals too, such as usa.gov. If portals were the main entrance to the Web (e.g. a place of discovery) in the 90s, search engines took their place around the turn of the century and dethroned entirely by social media after 2010.

Cloud storage and participative portals
The Cloud is an innovation linked with the Web 2.0 era. The Cloud is essentially storage space online that a person can rent or purchase to host their digital files. The files stored on the Cloud will be accessible from anywhere, from any device, as long as there is an Internet connection.

Since their inception, cloud services such as Dropbox and GoogleDrive have grown to encompass a suite of tools that make working online far easier. These tools include text and image-editing capabilities, collaborative tools (chat, version control) and secure backups and restore functions.

Collaboration across physical borders is one of the main attractions of cloud capabilities. As there are a growing drive and desire for designers to work outside of traditional office set-ups, all they need is a WiFi connection and the ability to share a virtual space with collaborators. With tools such as GitHub, designers can work from several locations, and all feed into the same files. Changes can be viewed instantly, and versions can easily be tracked back should problems occur. This way of working has led to flexible team working that can be structured project to project, and designers are free from the shackles of fixed office space and the associated costs.

One area of concern in regards to the Cloud is the encroachment on people's privacy. Every file a person stores online can be indexed, and the owner of the Cloud platform can sell information to third parties that is gained through a knowledge of the type of files you have stored.

News services (and rich media)
Cable television brought about 24-hour news and greater immediacy when reporting, and the Internet has exacerbated this further. Online news services now provide reporting on events as they happen. The route this reporting takes encompasses all the options that the Internet and rich media have to offer. Stories may be tweeted, or shared through apps alerting users to major events; videos can be uploaded in an instant, and the quality of images captured on mobile devices means that news can be reported from within an event by people on the ground.

The ability to report from the ground, coupled with the ability for anyone to share their opinion through a blog or social media, has led to a rise in citizen journalism. Many mainstream news services originate content from these non-traditional sources as it is quicker and easier than putting a journalist on the ground. This approach does come with its own set of problems. Verifying news as it happens is not an easy task, and many events have been misreported because each news network wants to be the first to report on a major story.

Media sharing websites and content platforms

A media sharing website is a site that enables users to upload, store, archive, share and curate their multimedia files (photos, videos, sound, music) with and for others.

Sometimes a media sharing website have some social functionality: each user has a profile, followers can comment and express admiration in just one click, users can send private messages but also curate content and build collections and channels. Furthermore, these sites have a standardised way of presenting sets of data: the use of a grid is very noticeable. Since the main purpose of a media sharing site is sharing, it also includes a search engine. Media stored on these sites can be embedded on other web pages.

Some media sharing websites, such as Storify, offer content curation, while others offer content creation such as Prezi, Issuu and Visual.ly. Some of these platforms disseminate content interspersed with advertising as a way of generating income.

Importantly, as a designer, you can use these platforms to promote your work.

VLE

VLEs, or Virtual Learning Environments, are spaces online that store and disseminate educational materials including videos, text documents, assignments, and so on. These spaces also allow students to take tests, upload projects, check for plagiarism and more. The plagiarism checker is possible because most of the texts ever released are now available online and therefore, they can easily be checked against any essay.

Several free alternatives have been developed in recent years. MOOCs (Massive Open Online Courses) hark back to the early intent of the Internet – to provide everyone with free, unlimited access to information. MOOCs strive to connect learners, and while there are free and paid for models, they tend to utilise freely available resources such as social media channels.

Beyond these examples, several video classrooms have been developed, such as lynda.com, teamtreehouse.com and skillshare.com. These services allow users to develop new knowledge and skills away from larger educational systems. Users can drop in and take a very particular class – this is especially useful for people in the workplace wanting to upskill.

Hosting

Once you've created a website, it needs to be stored somewhere that it is readily accessible at all times. Hosting servers are places where you can rent space to store your files (though many larger companies purchase their own) and point your URL to.

Hosting servers

There are generally two types of hosting servers: shared and dedicated. A shared server is exactly what it sounds like – you will rent a certain amount of space on a platform that you share with others. For a small company, shared hosting is fine, but it is less secure, and if one of the companies you are sharing with is hacked or attacked, it can affect your site. Dedicated hosting is more secure, but also much more expensive and requires more maintenance.

When you rent a space server, be sure that it matches your technical requirements; some cheap web hosting services do not accept WordPress installation, or allow you to run PHP (Hypertext Preprocessor), limit the video streaming debit or restrict the number of subdomains you could add.

What you should pay attention to when you look for renting a space server is the storage space (for example, is 500Gb enough if you want to store big video files?), the bandwidth (how much data are you going to upload to your space and how much you think your visitors are going to download to their browser?) and if the domain name renting is included in the hosting package.

Be aware that you do not own your space server; it is as if you were renting an apartment you will pay for once a year (or more, depending on the package you signed for; sometimes it is cheaper to rent it for five years, for example). You will be responsible for the content you store on the space server.

Control panel

The control panel is the online interface that allows you to access the hosting space and perform such operations as upload files, create (and check) email accounts, install databases and more. You can also upload and manage files on your server by using an FTP (File Transfer Protocol) client.

You may also use the server to host and manage CMS (Content Management Systems) applications such as WordPress. To do this, you will need to make sure PHP is installed on the server (to run WordPress), and you have the ability to create and access SQL (Structured Query Language) databases so that content can be created and stored.

Some hosting clients offer a domain name in addition to the space server; this will be explored in the next section.

URLs: Domain names and subdomains

A URL always begins with a protocol name such as HTTP (Hypertext Transfer Protocol) or HTTPS (Secure Hypertext Transfer Protocol), followed by the domain name and, in most cases, the name of the page or document that will be displayed in the browser's address bar.

By convention, the home/landing page of a website is called index.html. This name does not appear in the URL bar of the browser, though; for example, `mynicewebsite.com/index.html` will redirect automatically to `mynicewebsite.com`. Other documents or pages can be accessed by putting the complete URL in the browser bar, as long as you know the whole path that leads to it, and as long as permissions are in place; for example, `mynicewebsite.com/about.html`, `mynicewebsite.com/styles.css` or `mynicewebsite.com/images/myniceheader.jpg`.

A server room in one of Google's data centres

The Worldwide Web is essentially data, and as it grows, a massive, ever-expanding amount of data storage is required. The data stored needs to be constantly accessible and while terms like 'the cloud' imply this data is floating weightlessly, these servers are a very real representation of the physical space required for storage.

Image credit: Google

Cooling technology inside Google's data centres

These pipes transfer the water that keeps the servers cool. Google's servers are running constantly, and therefore could overheat if they are not cooled.

Image credit: Google

The path complexity depends on the structure of your website and on the technical framework you use. For example, a hand-coded website will have a different structure to a WordPress one. The places where your uploaded images, HTML pages and CSS files will be stored depend on the conventions adopted by the developer.

IP address, domain name and domain name registrar

On the Internet, each connected device has a unique identifier, an Internet Protocol (IP) address such as 192.0.2.23; since it is connected to the network, the hosting server you rent for your website has an IP address. On the World Wide Web, to make the location of your website more memorable and easier to access, and to make your URL 'cleaner', a domain name (such as example.com) is made up of two standard characters labelled and mapped to the IP address of your hosting server. The first label should not be longer than 63 standard characters without special characters, spaces or punctuation, such as 'example'; the second label is necessarily a TLD (Top Level Domain) such as '.com,' '.co.uk.' or '.org.'

The most common type of TDL is .com, and it is intended for commercial companies as opposed to organisations with tech interest (.net), charities (.org), governmental departments (.gov) and many others specific to certain countries (.co.uk, for example, is intended for companies based in the UK – these are called country code top-level domains).

You can rent a domain name from a domain name registrar who is accredited by the ICANN (Internet Corporation for Assigned Names and Numbers), based in the US.

If you rent your domain name and your space server from the same accredited company, it will link your domain name to your space for you. If you rent your domain name and space separately, you will have to redirect your domain name (example.com) to the IP address of your space server (192.0.2.23). There is a control panel on your domain name registrar website where you can assign the IP address given by your hosting provider to your domain name.

Be aware that you do not own your domain name; you will have to renew each year or more, depending on your contract (again, it may be cheaper to take a five-year engagement).

Subdomain

A subdomain is a domain that is part of a bigger domain, such as portfolio.example.com

A subdomain is partially dependent on its domain. It is useful when you want to create a new website on the same hosting server without having to rent or register a new domain name.

You can manage subdomains from the control panel of your hosting provider website.

The term URL (Uniform Resource Locator) will be familiar to most users of the Internet. Essentially, this is an address, or unique reference, that when entered into a browser's address bar will lead to a particular file or page on a person's hosting server. Each document on the Web has it own unique URL, whether displayed on a website or only stored on a person's hosting server.

URI

A URL is a specific type of URI (Uniform Resource Identifier), and this is used for documents accessed through a browser. You may use other URIs, such FTP (File Transfer Protocol), when using a client to upload files to a host server, and mailto when creating a link that will launch a user's default mail client.

Transferring data

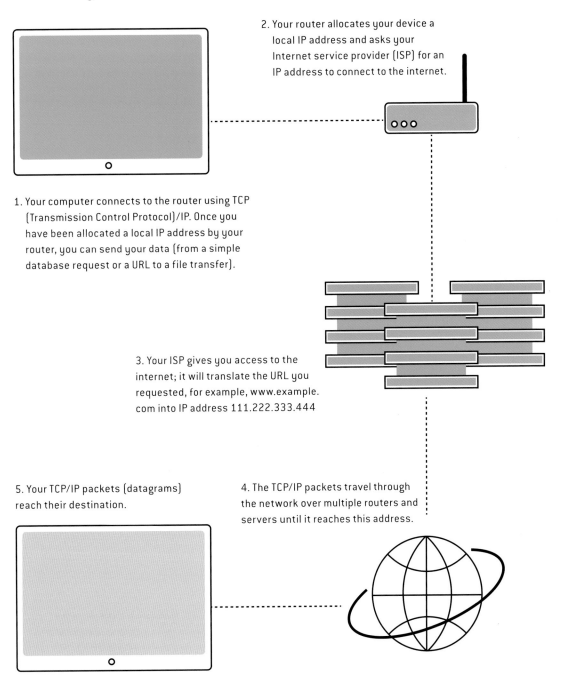

2. Your router allocates your device a
   local IP address and asks your
   Internet service provider (ISP) for an
   IP address to connect to the internet.

1. Your computer connects to the router using TCP
   (Transmission Control Protocol)/IP. Once you
   have been allocated a local IP address by your
   router, you can send your data (from a simple
   database request or a URL to a file transfer).

3. Your ISP gives you access to the
   internet; it will translate the URL you
   requested, for example, www.example.
   com into IP address 111.222.333.444

5. Your TCP/IP packets (datagrams)
   reach their destination.

4. The TCP/IP packets travel through
   the network over multiple routers and
   servers until it reaches this address.

Meet the designers: Tell us about yourself

Inayaili de León

I started working as a web designer in Portugal, where I grew up, about 15 years ago. I had the dream of moving to London since I was a teenager, and eventually got a job at a small digital agency here. I've done a bit of everything, from visual design, user experience, front end development (mainly HTML and CSS), and even print design, but my official role has always been as a designer. I also frequently write on my blog and other publications and speak at conferences internationally.

Bruce Lawson

I got into computers at school, because programming the school's 8K RAM computer in BASIC meant I could miss Physical Education classes. In 1999, I discovered the web, and now I advise companies, speak at events and train web developers to keep the web free, accessible and open. Previously I've been Deputy CTO at Opera Software, a tarot card reader in Istanbul, a volunteer pharmacist in Calcutta, tutor to a Princess' daughter in Bangkok, a musician, and a computer programmer.

Dan Hinton

I've always been someone who thought I could do anything if I put my energy into it. I enjoy working on multiple projects and businesses at the same time, getting a buzz from the fast-paced nature of the digital world. What I love most about the world we live in right now is how easy it is to be entrepreneurially minded. You have an idea, you can start something up there and then.

Ricky Gane

I'm Ricky Gane and I've been in the industry for over twelve years. I'm a fan of clean typography, hand-lettered signs and tattoo-style graphics. In my spare time I love fixing things up (old BMXs, Mk 1 Golfs...). When I'm not doing that, I'm spending time outdoors: riding my bike, out on the kayak or adventuring in our camper van. The thing I love about motion graphics and design is that there is always something new to learn.

Sush Kelly

I am a freelance designer/developer working mainly in the digital space. I have nearly twenty years agency experience, having helped nurture and develop a studio which I guess is what caused me to have such a broad range of interests. Currently I split my time between assisting a local agency in a lead/management role half the week and my own projects the rest of the time. I love pen and ink, drawing, and screen printing, so I dabble in this for fun.

Sylvie Daumal

I'm design director at WeDigitalGarden, an innovation agency created in 2016, but I have been working in the digital field for twenty years. I started designing CD-ROMs in the 90s and websites from 2000. In 2005, I discovered the user-centred approach. I worked for two agencies in Paris: Duke Razorfish and af83. I have been involved in the UX community since 2008 (EuroIA, UXCamp Europe) and created UX Paris group in 2009.

Ross Chapman

I'm a digital product designer and Head of Design Sprints at Etch, a design agency. I facilitate Design Sprints with teams, teach them how to use the framework and create content around it to support the community. I've been a designer for over a decade, and have worked at companies including Wiggle and Ericsson, with some freelance work too.
I love finding out how businesses work, understanding the people involved, and helping them work better together. I'm also a keen cyclist.

Nodesign

Nodesign is an award-winning design studio founded by Jean-Louis Frechin in 2001 and focused on innovation and technological creation. Pioneer of digital design, Nodesign is a recognised expert in new products such as: 'Connected Objects', 'Beautiful Interfaces', 'New Fabrications', 'Data' and 'Urban Design'. Ours is a strategic design that thinks of creation beyond the simple product.

Amy Parker

I'm currently Head of Design for a startup called Quala. Prior to this, my partner and I ran our own studio called Fore Design, focused on providing top-quality work to small businesses and startups. Though my formal training was in graphic design and my first job was in environmental design, I love being able to shift focus from branding and identity to interface to communications and copywriting.

Jamie Homer

I trained in the late 90s at Taunton's Somerset College of Art and Technology. At that point the Internet was still relatively in its infancy – as a consumer commodity at least. My training was in ideas-based traditional brand design. It had a strong focus on typography, which has since turned into a major and ongoing obsession!

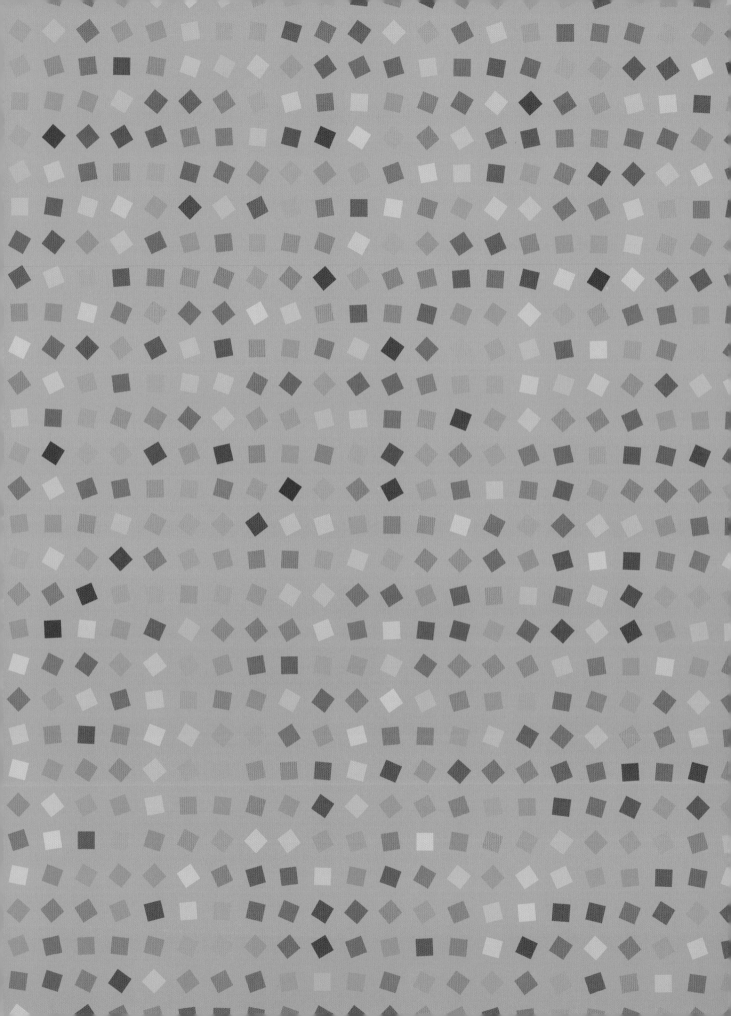

CHAPTER 2:
THE PROCESS

Designing for print is a reasonably linear process when compared to the journey of a project intended for a digital outcome. Once a document is sent to print, it is not often revised and revisited; when a digital solution is deployed, it will undergo a steady metamorphosis and be nurtured over time to ensure it reaches its full potential. This mode of thinking can be an adjustment for those who have worked in print, branding, etc. Throughout this chapter you will be introduced to methods of developing outcomes that can speed up the design process and help you make sure the right decisions are being made. We will discuss the ways which you can get to know your audience, test solutions, keep up to date with developments and plan your way through projects.

The brief

Often, a client comes to you with a need, not a brief. It is your job to work with the client to make sure they clearly define their business development needs, and to make sure you are prepared to put a solution in place that will help the client achieve these aims.

When defining objectives, the client will always want their business to grow, but you will need to work out the best way for them to achieve this. Merely having a website (or improving an existing website) will not help. Having clear site objectives will help a client reach their desired outcomes and clearly define the brief: do they need a calling card, a portfolio, an e-commerce site, etc.?

If the client is unsure of their exact objectives, you might start by looking at the competition and what they are doing well, or areas of business that they are not currently covering. You could also start by defining the budget as this will guide exactly what you can offer the client in terms of hours, processes and technology. For example, a client with a limited budget may require a templated solution, but a client with a larger budget could afford a completely bespoke service.

Additionally, in terms of your involvement, you will need to set expectations for the project. Being clear about what you will offer, and how you intend to do it will help avoid confusion later on. It is important that you are very specific about the services you will offer, as the client will not always understand the design process, or how long services will take: when offering to implement a brand across a website, make sure the client isn't expecting you to do the branding job as well because this is a service in itself.

Time scales and budget

It is important to deal with money upfront. However, knowing how much to charge a client when you are new to the business can be difficult. One suggestion is to consider how many hours you think the job will take, then multiply this by your ideal hourly rate. Do an idiot check — does this sound too cheap or too expensive? Build in a contingency. If you are unsure, ask other developers.

Get a clear brief and determine exactly what you can offer for what price — make it clear that extras will be charged for. Next, set deadlines for your client for deliverables, offering feedback, etc. Break down deliverables and give the client a timescale for delivery.

Give realistic timescales — if you think a job will take a day, tell the client to expect the work in three days. There will always be issues and hold-ups. It's better to surprise the client with an early delivery than disappoint them with a late one.

Offer amend stages — have specific times you will sit down with the client to talk through the site, otherwise, you run the risk of receiving emails and phone calls every time the client has a new thought.

Defining the brief and determining resources

Image over: designers at wedigital.garden involved in the critical planning and sketch stage of a project.

www.wedigital.garden

Needs of the client

Ensure your work meets the needs of the client — it's not about your interests and likes. The client is paying you, and everything you do should be to their benefit, even if this means politely letting them know their ideas might not work.

Always keep the client informed. Consider the start of a job as entering a partnership — it helps to think of the client as a colleague, as you should maintain similar levels of contact. You don't need to keep the client apprised of every change and issue, but if you are taking the project offline for a short amount of time, the client should know about this. Also, as mentioned before, make the client aware if there are issues that will affect the timeline and slow deployment.

It is important that you are fully aware of the client's expectations and goals. Looking at other websites is a good way of gauging this, as occasionally a client may not be able to verbalise their thoughts, or may not be aware of the possibilities.

Try to have a prototype that the client can regularly check-in on, and if you do this, alert the client when you are updating so they know to check in. A number of changes you will make may not be visible, or to the client may look very minor (even if you've worked through the night to achieve them!), so it is useful to offer some commentary and context as things progress.

The client needs to understand the design process — it's not as automated as many will expect! You will often need to let the client know how much time and skill goes into making the smallest element perfect and justify this by explaining the effect on the end-user. While some may not see the need to pursue clear consistency in design, the client will understand the monetary effect it will have on their business if the end-user cannot navigate the site smoothly, or find a contact form.

When negotiating amend and approval stages, make it clear how difficult and time-consuming undoing work and making changes might be. Again, some clients will think the process is more automated than it actually is and therefore be unaware of the finer complexities and associated time.

Process when working with a client
An ideal project flow; however, the reality is this rarely goes smoothly as client's priorities change, technologies are developed and discontinued, better solutions are found, and life happens!

PROCESS WHEN WORKING WITH A CLIENT

RESEARCH CLIENT & COMPETITION
—
MEET CLIENT
—
DEFINE/REFINE BRIEF
—
» PROTOTYPE » « TEST « »
—
» REFINE » « TEST « »
—
» DEPLOY » « TEST »
—
HAND OVER TO CLIENT
—
DEBRIEF CLIENT
•

Needs of the user

Beyond business needs, the end-user will have needs the client may not know about. There will also be technical considerations that may sound like technical jargon but are essential to the running of a modern website. It is important for the designer to highlight these requirements and educate the client, otherwise, the client may face problems later on – and the designer will likely be blamed!

Firstly, talk to the end-users as much as you talk to the client. The client thinks they know what their audience needs, but the end-user knows. You should converse with a range of people to get a spread of experience, reading and access levels, ability and knowledge of the client. This will give you an insight that will help make the site suitable for all. Ask them directly, what does the end-user really need? Some designs may only need a clear contact form!

You should always design for multiple platforms, as most websites will be viewed on mobile devices or tablets rather than traditional desktops computers and laptops.

Accessibility has always been a consideration when creating web content, but not one a layperson will be aware of. All web content

should be accessible to all people, regardless of disability. Site readers will be used by many people who are blind or partially sighted – this is technology that reads back the content of a page, and the reason why all text should be presented at textual content, not as an image file.

Ensuring readability of the content is not just the job of the client or a copywriter. The designer should test whether line lengths are reasonable, whether the content is free from jargon, and easy to digest and whether the content can be read in the average amount of time people spend on a given page (hint: this normally isn't very long at all).

Legibility is a major consideration, not just for people with sight impairments and disabilities, but for all people who wish to clearly read information on a page. Body and small text should be presented on a background away from images, and there should be adequate contrast to ensure the text is fully visible. This does not mean that all sites should have white background and black text, but there should be a good degree of contrast – in fact, many people with dyslexia find it much easier to read coloured text on a coloured background.

Needs of the designer

Too many designers put themselves last when it comes to working through a project, however, the designer is an active participant and should be rewarded as such. Conversely, far too many clients undervalue any service provided by a designer and will actively try to pay as little for design services as possible. This may be because the general populace see creativity and 'art' as something a person does for fun, and surely that should be a reward in itself?

A clear brief is absolutely essential for all parties. Never start a job until you know exactly what the client requires. More often than not, you are the best person to tell the client and write their brief for them, so do not worry about doing this – as long as they sign off the final draft!

One of the main reasons for getting a clear brief is so that you are able to give a realistic quote that relates to the amount of work you are about to undertake. In order to quote you will need to work out the amount of hours the job will take, and whether there are likely to be any other expenses such as calling in another designer to assist with the workload, or specialist equipment you will need to buy for the job.

Beyond this, payments from your client should arrive on time. No matter how much you may enjoy your job, you have bills and expenses. This is a job and you should be paid fairly within a specific time (normally thirty days). You also have the right to ask for some payment upfront to cover initial costs, and it is highly recommended that you do this with large jobs, or clients you are slightly wary of.

Lastly, you owe it to yourself to keep your knowledge relevant and current. Try to take time to learn and develop new skills. You will always learn on a job when there are problems, but this development is reactive – put aside time for deeper learning and properly immerse yourself in code.

The planning and development stage of a project

Image above: An active studio at wedigital.garden. As the planning stage of a project continues, prototypes and ideas are user-tested, and the designers start to settle on the best approach.

www.wedigital.garden

Research methods

There are many ways you may go about researching a web or digital project, and many things that you may research. As much as you need to research and know your technical skills, you also need to fully understand the people you are designing for – the client and end-user.

So, how do you get to know the people that will use the product or service you are developing?

Firstly, talking to the client and their end-users is a good way to gain an understanding of their ability, knowledge and expertise. Round table discussions, surveys and questionnaires are all useful ways of gathering knowledge. If you have a small group of people to speak to, a chat around a table is a good way to gather in-depth knowledge and uncover things you may not have expected. For larger groups of people, a questionnaire or survey can be sent by email, or completed through a web portal. This will give you greater amounts of data to analyse, but you will often lose the personal anecdotes that you may gain from a face-to-face discussion.

Traditional idea generation tools, such as mind mapping, are of course, as useful when designing for the Web as they are for any other creative project. Using techniques such as introducing random words and input will help you think about the project in a different and unique way (but what if it were blue? What if up was down?). You may rephrase the question to think about the client's needs from a different way ('we need more customers' might become – 'how do we make better use of our customer base?', or 'what would

we need to do to lose customers?'). You might look to break apart the problem ('what exactly are the elements that need to be completed?'), consider appropriation ('what can you make of the things around you?'), or when in dire need for inspiration, you might go off on a complete tangent and play a game of free association.

Once you have conducted this initial research, you may develop user scenarios – these will help you understand and express the reasons why a person might come to the website you are developing, what they will expect once they arrive, and how they will interact with the pages.

At this point, you should also look to survey competitors. Consider what they are doing right, and what you can learn from them. Also, think about what you may improve on. The competitor websites will also indicate the likely level of expertise your audience will have and what they will expect from the experience.

Once you have some working models, you will likely need to test them. This testing can be achieved informally by sitting people in front of a screen and asking then simple, direct questions about their journey and experience. Beyond this, user experience labs have the ability to track eye movements and the user's ability to navigate your designs. Here, you can more thoroughly test readability, legibility and flow of the navigation.

Approaches

As new technologies are developed, the approaches to using them also develop, as do the processes through which they are employed. The jobs of a designer and developer can be very different, but advances in technology – and a greater number of designers willing to learn markup language and code – has meant that a project workflow can be simplified and more tasks can be conducted by fewer people, simultaneously.

Agile working

A traditional web or digital workflow would fence off each part of the job. Once each section is complete it will be handed to the next person in the queue to do their bit (for example, a senior colleague might generate an idea, then a graphic designer interprets this and creates a page layout, they then hand the design to the developer, and then someone else tests the outcome). Ideas are fed forwards, and problems are then fed back. In terms of collaboration and timescales, this is not always the best way to work.

Agile working does away with a lot of these unnecessary divisions inherent in classic design studios, and elements are developed in unison: while one person is developing and testing wireframes, others will be hard at work on UI, UX, copy, etc., at the same time. Discovery happens the same time as design and everything is tested throughout the process. The team will work on a live test site, test as they go, and then modify as needed.

Another bonus of this way of working is seeing the customers as collaborators and as part of the process. Rather than staring at a PSD file, wondering how it will look in a browser, the client may assess functionality and style tiles at the same time, offering feedback and assistance along the journey.

Outsourcing and collaboration

With large and difficult jobs, don't try to do everything yourself.

Even beyond the traditional front end and back end division, no one person can develop every aspect of a digital project single-handedly. Depending on the size and type of job, some specialities will likely have to be sought out as the range of expertise required will often go far beyond photography and code – it may include copywriting, photography, illustration, marketing, SEO, film and more.

Network and try to surround yourself with a good team. If you know the right people, this, above all design skills, can make you a valuable resource!

Audience

The designer is not the audience, and the client is not the end-user. While you are working to a brief that matches the business objectives of the client, it is vital that you do not lose sight of the fact that your are designing for the people who will eventually use the site.

The client will make demands, and it is your job to understand which options and functions will genuinely benefit the design. Sometimes the best way to satisfy your client is to remind them that the person that matters most is the end-user, and then clearly demonstrate how your proposed options will positively affect their experience.

It is important that you know the end-user as well as the client so you can create outcomes that are fit for them. Therefore, you should try to meet these users – run a focus group, test your solutions, view users as they experience and navigate your designs. If you can get end-users to back up your assertions, this proves your worth and knowledge to the client, and results in establishing trust.

If you can't get the design for the end-user right, the client will not be able to meet their objectives for growth, increased sales or greater market presence.

Primary, secondary and tertiary users

All websites will have multiple groups of users. Each type of user will have different needs and requirements and normally, these can be grouped as primary, secondary and tertiary users.

If we take an example of a website that sells jeans aimed at teenagers, you will clearly see how one design must appeal to different demographics and not alienate any.

Primary users

As stated, the primary audience for this site is teenagers. When looking for jeans they will likely browse a number of pages, so yours needs to have impact, be relevant to their broader interests, and incite desire. For a teenage audience it will likely have to be edgy, anti-authority and not look like a site their parents would look at!

You should also consider the following: What devices do teenagers use? How long do they spend online, and on a given website? Is a website the best choice, or would advertising/placement on a social media site be more effective?

Secondary users

While the product and site are each aimed at teenagers, young people often do not have great spending power or a credit card. Adults will likely be the ones parting with their cash, so you also have to consider their needs. They will need to be confident in the payment systems, so use a recognisable brand for this and make it clear that the site is secure.

While the design needs to be edgy enough to attract the core primary users (teenagers), perhaps avoid imagery and copy that would put off the paying customer.

Tertiary users

This group are the hardest to define, as it could be anyone. Who else might happen upon the page? Grandparents? Pinterest pinners? Other designers?

As much as you can, try to consider these other users and make sure the design is approachable, usable and accessible to all.

Personas / usage scenarios

A good way of giving the end-user a relatable face is by drawing up a persona. Your audience may be massive, and this method allows you to focus on an individual; then, through this, find a focus for the project that can be shared with your team. Once you start talking about the persona, it removes all hint of the designer's personal choice, and it makes it about the person you have created.

The first rule of drawing up a person is to be as thorough as possible – you should consider all parts of their lives, from spending power to place of employment, and number of children to hobbies and interests. Where do they go at the weekend? What's their favourite restaurant? Of course, you will need to conduct some research to answer all of these questions, and that will involve talking to your client's current or intended audience.

Conducting this type of research is a good way to get the client involved, and the picture that emerges is useful to refer back to during the project when you are stuck or want to test a concept.

Once you know who the audience is, you will want to consider how they might use the platform you are developing. If you can, it is useful to observe how and when your audience access their digital devices – do they check email on the bus with their smartphones, or are they desktop only types? Do they sit in front of the TV with a tablet every evening, or do they prefer a break from digital interactions when they are at home?

You should consider the level of proficiency your end-user is likely to have – are they tech savvy, or do they still write all of their passwords in a notebook? View your intended audience to ascertain the sort of problems might they come up against when using the new platform – will they know what a hamburger menu is? How able are they to read text on the screen (and also, what amount of text can they read on the screen?).

Think about how the user will find the site in the platform in the first place. Will it be through traditional word of mouth, search engines, social media, or is it something that requires a download or plug-ins, etc.?

To answer all of the above, you also need to understand competitors' sites. View your audience using their platforms – what are they doing right and what can you do better?

Who is your audience?
Challenge briefs that are aimed at limited audiences – the world will have access to your designs, and the solutions should (ideally) be global.

Idea generation

Idea generation is not only helpful when you are stuck; as a tool, it's also useful to challenge the things you know, and your assumptions about how things should be done. The initial stages of a project should be as thorough as an archeological dig or a forensic examination – you should start a project by looking for clues in the brief, dusting off the assets you are given, delving into your tool kit to find the best way of approaching the job, and, most importantly, of all weighing up and challenging the evidence.

The important word here is evidence. Your ideas are one thing, but how do you really know you are right? Even if your design scenarios feel fit for purpose, you should look to challenge these by tweaking your aesthetic choices, removing and adapting code to find the leanest build, and turning the brief on its head to see what else emerges.

There are idea generation processes you can go through and games you can play, which go far beyond basic spider diagrams.

Challenging associations

For each key word on the brief, consider what you associate with it, what the client may think, and what the end-user is likely to understand from it. Do the words suggest colours, emotions, copy choices, particular functions or functionality?

When you have a new list of words, pull these together and perhaps run the activity once more. Each time you do this, new ways of approaching the brief will emerge.

Mood and concept boards

Again, as you examine the brief make a note of the visuals it suggests. Try to find examples of these visuals in old magazines, or photocopy pages from books. Once you have a range of visual references start to collate these onto boards. Once you have a few boards, step back and see what the collections suggests – you might find patterns that suggest new approaches.

Additionally, when you are visualising your ideal end-user (creating a persona) think about the visual material they will engage with on a daily basis – the brands they like, the clothes they might wear, etc. You might want to make sure your design fits next to the other elements in their life, or you may wish to challenge the patterns and make something that stands out.

Appropriation and bricolage

Appropriation is the art of using what is around you to create new work. While you should not use the work of others without permission – and you cannot use work that you have submitted to another client – every designer ends up with a huge a stockpile of unused colour palettes, references and tutorials that can be used for current and future projects.

Similarly, bricolage is the process of looking at past experiences. While this is obvious to a point (you don't relearn HTML for every web project) some designers tend to reinvent the wheel every time a new project surfaces. Much like the pile of visual references you already have, are there common bits of code you can reuse, or basic page structures that can form the architecture of new work?

Lateral thinking

Lateral thinking is the process often referred to as 'thinking outside the box'. If you simply accept the knowledge presented to you by other designers and developers, you will never innovate and create new paths. You should always challenge the common ideas that surround

designing for Web and digital – approach every problem with the thought that you are going to improve on past and current work, not copy others'. Ask 'why' at every stage and be critical of the solutions presented to you. There is always a better way of doing things.

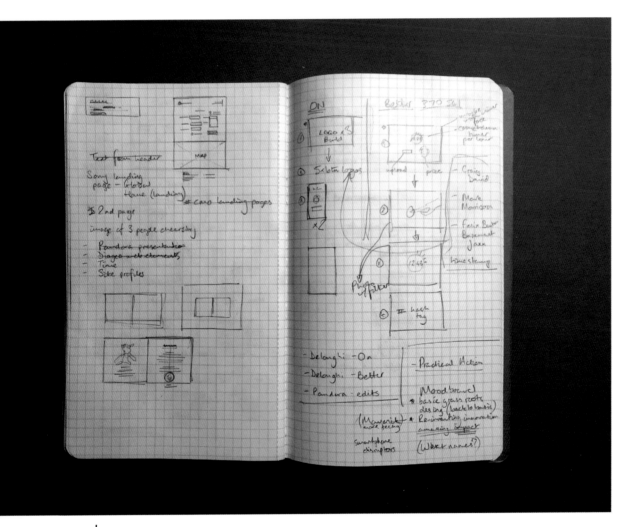

The humble sketchbook

Image above: The sketchbook of designer Jamie Homer. While Jamie works with a range of digital tools, all of his projects start with quick sketches, notes from the clients and a collection of ideas and possibilities.

www.jamiehomer.co.uk

Six Thinking Hats

If you are working in a team, there are joint ideas exercises that you can pursue, such as the Six Thinking Hats process developed by Edward de Bono. Essentially, this is a game created to help you think outside of your normal patterns. Each player will be assigned a coloured hat, and this hat represents the problem they have to think about.

The coloured hats are used as follows:

- The white hat represents everything you need to know about a subject – only the facts, no emotions.

- The green hat stands for creativity. Green should investigate the problem and propose any provocations.

- The red hat is concerned with feelings and emotional responses.

- The yellow hat tries to find the positive in the arguments and propositions.

- The black hat plays 'devil's advocate' and looks for problems and flaws.

- The blue hat is worn by the chairperson of the meeting, and their task is to make sure that everyone is heard.

Designers using Google's Jamboard to collaborate and work up ideas

While many of the idea generation techniques discussed in this chapter are intended for teams working face-to-face, technology has now made it possible for people to collaborate virtually and remotely.

Image credit: Google

Brief to solution
The following visual shows an ideal idea generation and research process.

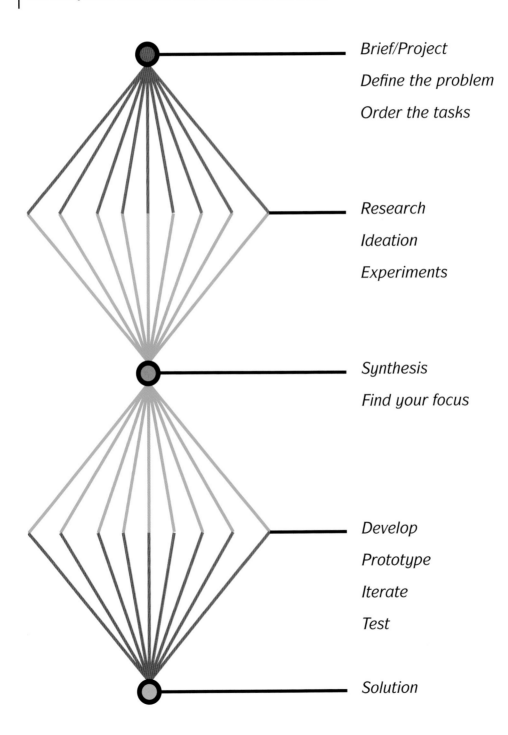

Brief/Project

Define the problem

Order the tasks

Research

Ideation

Experiments

Synthesis

Find your focus

Develop

Prototype

Iterate

Test

Solution

Staying informed (technology)

Working in the digital environments means that you are at the forefront of change and development, so how do you stay informed? You can read blogs, follow industry experts on social media, read trade publications and magazines, attend workshops and lectures, or even hang out with other people in your sector. You might find places to network with other designers and developers – this can be a good way of sourcing future collaborators.

It's useful to play and tinker with new technologies. You might take part in hack days or join open device labs that will allow you access to tools that are not otherwise accessible.

In terms of learning new skills that will enable you to take on a broader range of projects, you can access a number of online learning environments, but you might also attend hack events or hackathons. Normally, a hack event lasts for a day or two, and over this time you will develop something entirely new, without a brief or a client. This type of undirected design work will really allow you to think outside of the box and get to grips with a range of new skills.

Planning

If a project is to be successful, it requires careful and thorough planning. Poor planning leads to late work, and this leads to unhappy clients, so you cannot afford to approach a project without a clear idea of what you will be doing and when.

Most essentially, you will need to know how much time you will need to give the project, and when you can achieve this. Time is a clear indicator of what you can achieve and whether you need to outsource and bring people in.

The next level of planning is thinking about skills. Are you capable of creating every part of the project, or again, should you outsource?

Even if you choose to work alone, the project will need clear structure, objectives and aims, otherwise how will you know when the project is complete?

However, there will always be contingents that you cannot plan for, so give yourself some leeway and always aim to complete a project well ahead of time. If nothing does go wrong, you can take it easy for a few days!

Staying informed: design sprint
Image, this page and over: Ross Chapman running a design sprint (a time-constrained approach to the design process). A design sprint is a good way for design teams to develop prototypes quickly, test ideas, and consider a range of approaches, without using up great amounts of client and agency time. The lack of time encourages quick, agile thinking.
www.rosschapman.com

Sitemaps

Sitemaps are important from two points of view – they will help you understand the structure and hierarchy of the design, and they also help search engines understand how things are linked.

There are a few important factors you should consider when drawing out a site map. Chief amongst these decisions are which pages will be your top level of links (i.e. which pages are the most important and likely to be most visited), and how you will structure the links below the top level. You will need clear links to important pages – such as contact, about and home – but what are the next pages the user will visit?

Consider whether you will classify links using a drop-down menu system, or will you have subnavigation sections elsewhere on the page? Alternatively, you might offer different navigation systems depending on the section/page. A design

might feature a primary navigation in the header, a secondary navigation in a sidebar, and quick links in the footer.

The sitemap below, designed by Niccolò Miranda, offers little detail as to the design of the pages, but clearly indicates the title of each page, how it links from the main or secondary navigation, and what type of content it will likely contain.

The two-click rule is a bit antiquated but still a good guide. This rule states that a user should be able to reach any page on a site within two clicks. This might be possible for small portfolio sites, but for systems that are searchable and data driven, two clicks is near impossible. However, you still want to make navigation as easy as possible because people will click away quickly if they can't find the links and pages they want.

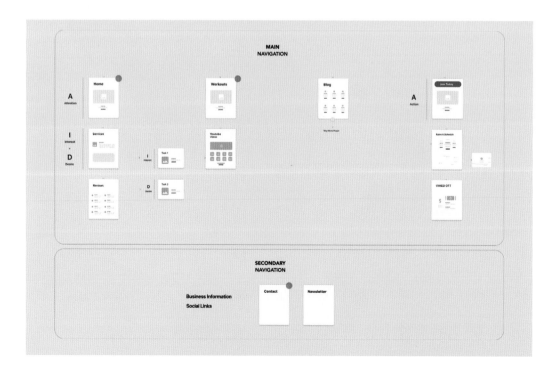

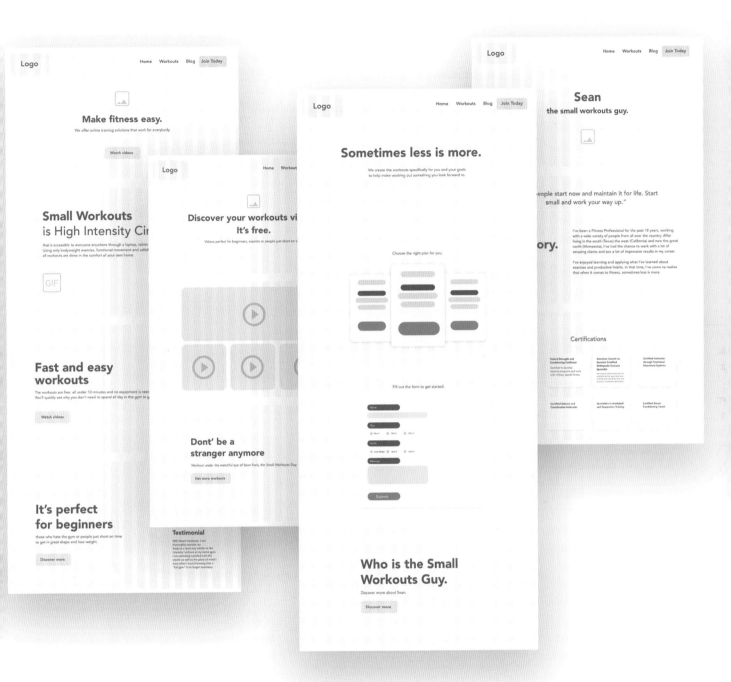

Niccolò Miranda

Small Workouts Website (images page 68 - 71)

If a sitemap provides the blueprint for your whole website, a wireframe represents the blueprint for a single page. This prototyping step allow you to establish the basic structure of the pages. Including content and digital copywriting, wireframes help to understand how to structure visual design.

www.niccolomiranda.com

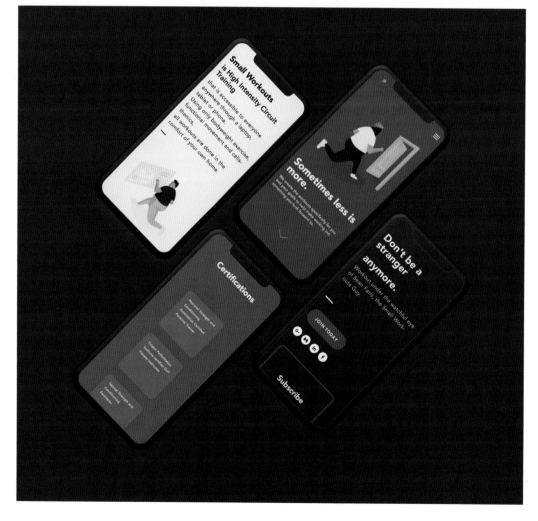

Niccolò Miranda

Small Workouts Website

Small Workouts, a remote fitness training business based in Minnesota, commissioned Niccolò Miranda to redesign their company website. He decided to use the AIDA in his web project. The AIDA is a process model used in marketing to sell a product or service, which involves getting a customer's attention. The four stages of AIDA include: Attention, Interest, Desire and Action.

The integration of AIDA into the sitemap (a diagram of the site hierarchy) has been designed to draw 'attention' through illustrations and animations, create 'interest' by showing the services to users, create 'desire' through photos of people in great shape, and finally the 'action' by clicking on "Join Today" button.

www.niccolomiranda.com

Development

The stages of development will vary depending on the job, but as a rough guide, the following is a standard flow. Please note, the flow is not linear – as with agile working practices, you will likely go back and forth through the stages until a satisfactory resolution is arrived at.

Wireframes

Wireframing is the initial starting point in the development of the screen designing process for the graphic designer. The process of wireframing is used to 'mock up' the initial layout, structure and placement of a website hierarchy of content, and can be produced either on paper through sketches or by using software that generates rough HTML layouts such as InVision, Mockflow, Justinmind, Flinto, Wireframe.cc, and more. The emphasis of this stage of development is to consider the elements required for the site, flow, behaviours, hierarchy and scale.

When developing the wireframe the content is structured in a series of shapes to inform the viewer where the content will be placed within the layout. The example shown opposite gives a visual representation of where images and text will be placed, alongside the basic structure of the navigation system.

Other wireframe content can include: contact forms, advertisements, video, animation or image galleries. Wireframe development and layout can change as the project progresses, and because of the ease of use in placing shapes, this means placement of content structure can be changed quickly and easily at the starting point of the design process.

Wireframing is an important first stage in the development of a website, because it allows the designer to plan the layout and interface without being distracted by content such as typefaces, colour or body copy.

There are a number of wireframing software tools available to the designer, which range from web-based online solutions to stand-alone applications. For users of the Adobe Creative Cloud applications, both Adobe InDesign and Illustrator can be used, with both pieces of software having the necessary tools to develop wireframes and a range of file formats to export to if print outs are required. There is quite a range of web-based software available. Some companies offer free trial versions, so this is a good starting point to see if the software is appropriate for your needs.

Balsamiq Mockups is a software that includes several drag-and-drop elements, from buttons to lists, each styled as a hand-drawing. The basic premise behind this wireframing tool is to keep the mock-ups 'intentionally rough and low fidelity', to encourage as much feedback as possible.

As well as creating mock-ups, Axure allows you to add functionality to your layout and create an interactive prototype. Features of this wireframing tool include sitemaps and various 'widgets' in the form of various UI elements. Interactive HTML mock-ups can be created for both websites and apps; you can even view your app design on your phone with a built-in share function.

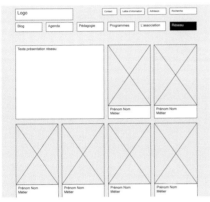

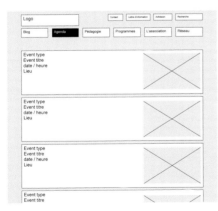

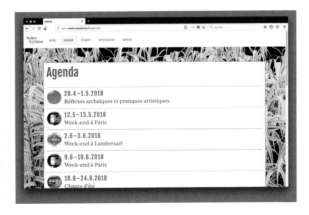

BANK Associates

Ateliers Solstices

(Left) Initial wireframe sketches compared to the final live design (right). As you can see in this comparison, when content is added to the design, it often becomes apparent that some elements need to be adjusted. However, the wireframe is a good start point as it offers a structure from the outset.

www.bankassociates.de

Sample content

When developing style tiles and wireframes, it is useful to have content to work with. Using live content will help you assess whether the choices you have made are the right ones; for example, the length of articles and pages might affect the way they are laid out, and if the client likes to use lots of visuals, you might avoid employing too many other clashing visual elements.

Style tiles

Style tiles are almost the opposite of wireframes – here you concentrate on graphical design elements (typographic choices, treatments of images, colour choices, etc.) and consider how this might eventually shape the design. While you will consider ideas of hierarchy, proportion and scale, you will do this away from the layout – essentially separating style, content, flow and presentation.

Style tiles are used as a visual reference of the website or application, and are similar to mood boards in some aspects of content. Style tiles build on the visual 'story' of the content, and begin to assign fonts, colour and style collections together. They can also include the elements of the navigation interface system; the client's brand and visual references to all of the elements combined can also be included. Style tiles should offer a clear starting point for discussion between the designer and the client, and clarification on the client's business goals and personal preferences.

For style tiles to be successful, initial meetings with the client should inform the designer of the client's needs and what they wish to achieve with the project, and any preferences the client already has for the design. As the development of the style tile progresses, alterations and edits from discussions with the client may take place before the final design solution style tile is in place.

Mock-ups and prototyping

Mock-ups and prototyping take the designer to the second stage in the developmental process, progressing from 'low-fidelity' wireframes to 'high-fidelity' layouts and designs.

Mock-up content is added (such as images, body copy and colour) and the design of the navigation is introduced. Alterations to the initial wireframes may need to be considered at this time, perhaps

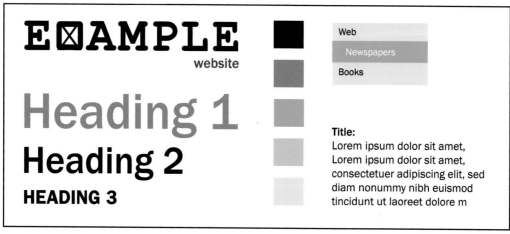

Sample style tile
An example of a (very) simple style tile.

due to amount of copy or image placement. Team and client feedback is important at this stage in the design process.

Until a few years ago, prototyping was not part of the designer's 'toolkit', as the software to create prototypes did not exist. The need for prototyping digital design came from both the designer and client's desire to see as close to a fully functioning website or application as possible. In the past, designers printed out static layouts, or clients viewed the designer's mock-ups on-screen, with no ability to interact with the navigation or content. Prototyping now allows this to happen, links between pages, and 'clickable' actions can be added to content to give a more real-world scenario to the overall design.

As prototyping has become important and popular within the design process, prototyping tools are becoming much more sophisticated

in their functions and ability to replicate interactive actions. Currently, the most popular web-based application for website and mobile application prototyping is InVision.

InVision is a web-based application, that allows designers to upload and add their own imagery, text and navigation system. The software prototypes a number of functions ranging from linking pages of website pages to simulating mobile phone applications such as sweeping left to right and scrolling. The InVision software allows the designer to collaborate online with others in the team, and to preview the prototype through a desktop browser or on a mobile phone using the InVision app.

If you are using the Creative Cloud apps, Adobe has launched its own prototyping software in the form of Adobe Experience. This works in the same was as InVision Experience and allows the designer most of the same options as InVision.

Mock-ups and prototyping

Image above: Designer Jamie Homer working with his team.

www.jamiehomer.co.uk

Testing

To fully demonstrate to a client how their website will look and feel, it is useful to have a live version on dev (development) server that the client can access and test. This is especially useful if you are working at a distance from the client and cannot physically meet to demonstrate changes.

Device and cross browser testing

If you start with wireframes, you can test rough HTML models from the outset. You should always test as thoroughly as possible as you don't want panicked clients calling you to say that the site doesn't work on the latest device!

User tests (UX)

As soon as you have something to test, you should test it. It is really useful to gather feedback as you develop rather than putting all of your efforts into a design, then realising that the users don't like it or can't use it.

However, make sure you hide the live version from the general public. The client may have time-sensitive information held within their pages, or they may simply not want the public to see the site until it is final. This cloaking can be achieved normally with a holding page, but for extra security you might want to give the client some login credentials.

The downside of working on a live server is that if your client has constant access, they will check for updates constantly. Unless you are working on one job at a time or making very obvious changes to the front end, the client can become frustrated with the lack of (visible) updates, so it can be useful to only give access at certain checkpoints.

Wireframes

Image above and over: Thorough planning at the wireframe stage of a project.

Photographs by Andrew Way and Alexander Lucas

Deployment

This is the part of the project that is occasionally followed by a few quick fixes, but more often than not, a few celebratory drinks!

Once a website is complete, it will need to be launched. Sometimes, this may be as simple as removing a holding page, but other times it may be more complicated.

If you have created a static HTML and CSS build, deploying may be as simple as using an FTP (File Transfer Protocol) client to connect to the web server and then replace the old files. Some programs, such as Dreamweaver, have FTP capabilities, but there are many stand-alone applications that will achieve the same, such as Fetch, CyberDuck and FileZilla.

Some websites are easily moved over from a dev space to their natural home, but if a database is involved, you may need to edit the entries to ensure that the pages are looking in the (new) right place. Thankfully, most database changes can be achieved with a text editor and a find-and-change.

One note about deployment – it's good to prepare the client and make them aware that it will take a while for their brand new site to hit search engines, and for new users to interact. Many clients have contacted their designer/developer a day after deployment wondering why they are not at the top of Google searches already.

Safe working practices

With website design involving working with computers for long periods of time, it is important that you sit in a way that does not harm your arms, back, hands, shoulders or neck. The following information offers some simple guidelines to help ensure that your work area is set up properly.

Problems caused by computer screens are usually the result of improper use rather than the screen itself. There is no evidence that screens damage eyes, but long periods of working at a computer screen can cause discomfort. You must ensure the text and images on the screen are the right size for you. You should also take regular breaks.

Discomfort while sitting – particularly in the back, neck, shoulders, arms and hands – can occur if you adopt awkward postures, repeatedly make the same movements, or don't vary your posture. To avoid any of these problems, making sure your chair is adjusted correctly for you is essential. When adjusting your chair, it can be useful to move it away from your computer, adjust it so that your feet are flat on the floor and there is not excessive pressure on the underside of your thighs, and then make the following adjustments:

- Your backrest should go up and down. You should adjust its height so that it supports you in the small of your back; the part of the backrest that sticks out most should fit into the small of your back (usually just above belt level). Experiment with the height of the backrest until you find what is most comfortable.

- Adjust the backrest angle so that your back is supported for all tasks that you are doing. You may need to readjust this during the working day depending on the length of time you are working on your computer.

- If you can tilt the seat, adjust it so that your hips are higher than your knees. A slight forward tilt helps to maintain a healthy shape in your back.

- If your chair has armrests, adjust these so that they comfortably support your elbows when your shoulders and upper arms are relaxed. They should not force you to sit with your arms away from your body, nor should they prevent you from sitting sufficiently close to your desk.

- Always try throughout your day to take regular breaks, stand up, walk around and focus away from the screen to rest your eyes.

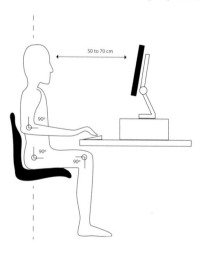

50 to 70 cm

Sheida Pourian
Motion Popi (page right)
An animation about working safely online.
www.behance.net/popisheida
www.behance.net/gallery/58139605/
POPIMotion-Graphics

Meet the designers: How would you describe your job?

Inayaili de León

I work on a design systems team and focus mostly on the documentation and process side of things. That means I need to be aware of all the design and front end engineering work that is done across the different teams that use the system. From there, I try to understand which components, guidelines and processes we need to create or change to improve the quality of the product itself. The design system is just like any other product: it needs to be improved, maintained, and documented.

Bruce Lawson

I work with organisations to help them make their products more compliant with web standards, bring it to market, advising on technical and developer relations strategy, and everything else.

Dan Hinton

I'm Creative Director for two companies. The more established Pixelfish is a digital design agency, so I'm working on websites predominantly – both the design and development. The newer business, named Hatch Apps, specialises in bringing people's ideas to life in the digital world – this one is at times very technical.

Ricky Gane

I'm a Motion Graphics Creative for a large advertising agency. My job role covers everything from creating conceptual storyboards, animating in After Effects, producing 3D visuals in Cinema 4D to video editing and colour grading. I come from a traditional print design background and try to bring those same design principles through when starting any new project.

Sush Kelly

Varied! Every day is different, as a freelancer, unless you have a very specialist skill set you can often find your work taking you into areas you may be a little weaker in. Having a really good learning ethic helps a lot. There are boring things to be done too such as your accounts, chasing invoices and also trying to get new work. I left agency work full time to try and address the balance of work/life so as much as possible stick to normal working hours, though it can be tempting to burn the midnight oil.

Sylvie Daumal

I manage the design team. I check the deliverables on a regular basis and follow the projects. My role is to ensure the quality of the outcomes, so I'm deeply involved in defining the methodology. I'm also involved in all the client-facing activities: I attend the user tests and, more general meetings. My main role is to decide which tools we use. It's not only the software, it's also user research, scenarios, workshops, prototyping or testing methods.

Ross Chapman

What I need from a job is variety, and enough autonomy and freedom to work on what I think is most important. I get that at Etch. Most weeks I'm running a design sprint with a team and when I'm not, I'm teaching others, or doing the necessary sales and marketing that any business function needs. Putting myself out there, making myself vulnerable and just doing it instead of planning it has been one of my key tactics in recent years.

Nodesign

Release beauty and good out of necessity and complexity.

Amy Parker

I handle anything and everything related to product and brand: product vision, prototyping, interface design, brand communications, and marketing.

Jamie Homer

I've worked really hard over the years to be in a position to work at what's called a portfolio career. It essentially involves dividing up your time amongst various roles and skills that you're good at and really enjoy, instead of being chained to a desk and soldiering on at one defined task all the time. It's made even easier with all the remote working capabilities offered by technology as well!

CHAPTER 3:
CODING AND MARKUP LANGUAGES

There is no one way to develop digital solutions. While the methods of production will normally be dependent upon the aim of the project and the desired outcome, there are still a number of ways any build can be approached. There are a variety of coding languages, and each of these has its own particular use. Whether or not you intend to design or develop the outcomes, it is useful to understand the flavour of the particular underlying codebase. Through this chapter, we will introduce you to the main languages that might be employed, discuss their usage, and offer some visual examples.

HTML

HTML, or Hypertext Markup Language, was developed by Sir Tim Berners-Lee. While some refer to HTML as code, and the act of writing HTML as coding, this is slightly deceptive. Being a markup language, the process is more akin to the way newspapers were developed before computers.

A long time before InDesign, a designer would create a layout for a page and determine rules for the hierarchy, presentation and style. The text would be submitted by a journalist, and a photographer or illustrator might provide some imagery. A typesetter would work to the rules of the designer and determine how many words might fit on a line, in a column, and on a page.

The way HTML functions is similar in many ways. Text and imagery are supplied to the designer and incorporated into a design. The designer writes certain rules (HTML combined with CSS), and the browser effectively does the typesetting, adhering to the rules dictated.

If you think of the design of a web page as being similar to a printed page, HTML is the raw content before the visual style is applied [we do this using CSS, and there is more about this on page 90]. HTML tells a browser what the content is and how to handle the various elements presented. For example, the following HTML tells the browser that a certain piece of text is a link, and also where that link will lead the viewer should it be clicked:

```
<a href="http://www.example.com/"
target="_blank">Link text goes here</a>
```

HTML is generally presented in one fashion (there are a few exceptions that we will come to). An opening tag tells the browser what an element is, and this helps the browser decide on the best way to handle and present that particular piece of content. Following the content, you will have a closing tag, and that tells the browser that this particular section is closed. Here is an example:

```
<h1>This is an example title</h1>
```

<h1> is the opening tag and this tells the browser that it is a heading. Being h1, the browser (and search engines) also understand that this is the most important header on the page. <h1/> closes this particular element and any styles or rules applied to this object will not be carried on to the next element.

One of the few exceptions for the opening and closing tag rule is the way images are referenced in the markup. Here you have no closing tag, and it contains attributes only. An example image tag is:

```
<img src="http://www.nameofsite.
com/img/image.jpg" alt="some text"
style="width:650px; height:350px;">
```

The source directs the browser to where the image is stored, and the alt text tells the search engine what the image content is; this can also be spoken back to users who are partially sighted via a screen reader. When you drop an image into an HTML editor, it will normally generate the style attributes; however, it is sometimes best not to define height and width if you are controlling these with CSS to create a flexible (responsive or adaptive) layout.

For more examples, see: www.wdgd.co.uk

Page basics

The HTML	What is this?
`<!DOCTYPE html>`	This is a doctype. This snippet tells the browser what type of document it is looking at so that the content can be correctly interpreted.
`<html> </html>`	These tags wrap around your page and essentially tell the browser where the visible (the body) and non-visible (the head) content begins and ends.
`<head> </head>`	The head section is not to be confused with the HTML5 header tag. The head holds non-visual material that enables the site's functions. You will place links to CSS files here, or perhaps JQuery libraries.
`<title> </title>`	This is the title of the page and it appears on the top bar of the browser window, and in your bookmarks.
`<body> <body>`	The body holds all of the visible content for your website. This is presented using various content markup and then displayed accordingly in the browser window.

An example of a basic page

```
<!DOCTYPE html>
<html>
<head>

<title>Title of the site goes here</title>

</head>


<body>

<h1>This is an example title</h1>
<h2>Secondary title</h2>
<p>Here is some text</p>
<a href="example.com" target="_blank">This is a link to site example.com</a>

</body>

</html>
```

Content markup

Example	The HTML	What is this?
This is one paragraph. This is another paragraph.	`<p>This is one paragraph.</p>` `<p>This is another paragraph.</p>`	The `<p>` tag surrounds each paragraph of text on your page. The `</p>` tag closes that section.
# This is the main...	`<h1>This is the main title of the page or website</h1>`	This is your main heading. It should be used once per page as it gives search engines a clue what the page is about.
## This is the title of an article or subsection…	`<h2>This is the title of an article or subsection, less important than H1, but more important than H3</h2>`	This is your secondary heading and can be used multiple times.
### This is the title, less important than H2, but more…	`<h3>This is the title, less important than H2, but more important than H4</h3>`	This is your tertiary heading and can be used multiple times.
This is the title, less important than H3, but more important than…	`<h4>This is the title, less important than H3, but more important than H5</h4>`	This heading can be used multiple times.
This is the title, less important than H4, but more important than H6	`<h5>This is the title, less important than H4, but more important than H6</h5>`	This heading can be used multiple times.
This is the title, less important than H5	`<h6>This is the title, less important than H5</h6>`	This heading can be used multiple times.
This is a link	`<a href="http://www.nameofsite.com/" target="_blank">This is a link</a>`	This is the default HTML styling of a text link and it can be styled using CSS.

Example	The HTML	What is this?
Strong	`<strong>Strong</strong>`	`<strong>` will make a word bold, but it can be styled to do otherwise.
Emphasis	`<em>Emphasis</em>`	To emphasise a word, use `<em>`. This applies italics, but it can be styled to do otherwise.
This word is red	`<p>This word is` `<span>red</span></p>`	`<span>` can be applied to make elements stand out in more bespoke ways. This needs to be styled with CSS.

1. Goat
2. Chicken
3. Cow
4. Hen
	`<ol>`
	`<li>Goat</li>`
	`<li>Chicken</li>`
	`<li>Cow</li>`
	`<li>Hen</li>`
	`</ol>`
		This is an ordered list. It presents content in a specific hierarchical way – this is normally visualised with A, B, C or 1, 2, 3 preceding each item.

• Goat
• Chicken
• Cow
• Hen
	`<ul>`
	`<li>Goat</li>`
	`<li>Chicken</li>`
	`<li>Cow</li>`
	`<li>Hen</li>`
	`</ul>`
		This is an unordered list, there is no implied order. It is normally visualised with discs or bullet points preceding each item.

This is a break	`<p>This is   a break` `</p>`	The ` ` is used to create line breaks. This is less commonly used in responsive and adaptive designs, and the line lengths vary depending on screen ratio.
_____	`<hr>`	This is a horizontal rule. It is used to break up content and can be styled using CSS.
	`<!-- This is a comment -->`	Comments can be used by the developer to add notes within their code – these only appear in the markup, and not as a visual element.
this & that	`<p> this &amp; that</p>`	This is an example of a HTML entity – several characters are reserved for use in HTML, so are substituted with a reference such as this when used in text.

HTML5

HTML5 was developed in the early 2000s. It is known for employing simplified terms and greater standardisation of tags. Largely, this simplification was a reaction to the way each designer was creating elements, such as sidebars and footers, all using different variations of div tags and classes (See more: Div id and class, page 92). HTML5 brought in tags such as:

`<header> </header>`

The header holds information such as the site logo, hero image, navigation section and prominent messaging. The header section should not be confused with the head section as that sits outside of the content that is visible.

`<nav> </nav>`

This tag holds the navigation links for the website. It often sits within the header section. Often the links held within the nav will be presented as list items (`<li> </li>`) in an ordered list (`<ol> </ol>`) or an unordered list (`<ul> </ul>`).

`<footer> </footer>`

The footer area sits at the bottom of the web page and holds content such as copyright information, social media links, quick links and 'small print' text.

`<main> </main>`

Use this tag only once per page. It should surround the most important information — the main content would be separate to the sidebars and footer elements.

`<article> </article>`

Used often for blog-style layouts when you have similar areas of content that repeat.

`<section> </section>`

You would use section to group an area of content — this grouping would normally include a heading and several other elements.

`<aside> </aside>`

Asides may be used in two different ways. In an article, the aside will group content that is linked to the main content, but aside from it. Also, many developers use the aside for sidebar content, normally coupled with a float element.

The opposite page includes an example blog-style layout that uses HTML5 to house and describes different types of content.

All visual elements are contained in the `<body>` while the `<head>` includes information required by the browser, such as the page name. The `<header>` includes important titling information.

Below this the `<main>` section contains the blog content subdivided into `<article>` sections, each with their own title.

After the `<main>` section, you will see an `<aside>` area that acts as a sidebar, and the `<footer>` houses copyright information.

[For more examples, see: www.wdgd.co.uk]

```
<!DOCTYPE html>
<html>
  <head>
    <title>Title of the site goes here</title>
  </head>
<body>
  <header>
  <h1>Name of the page</h1>
  <h2>Subheading</h2>
  </header>

<main>
  <h2>Title of this main area</h2>
  <p>Here is some text.</p>

<article>
  <h3>Title of the article</h3>
  <p>Here is some text</p>
</article>

<article>
  <h3>Title of the article</h3>
  <p>Here is some text</p>
</article>

</main>

<aside>
  <a href="example.com">This is a text link to the site example.com</a>
  <a href="example.com" target="_blank"> This is a text link to example.com
  that opens in a new window</a>
</aside>

<footer>
<h5>&#169; 2019</h5>
</footer>

</body>
</html>
```

HTML5
An example HTML5 page layout.

CSS

HTML works with the browser to display content, and CSS (Cascading Style Sheets) does the important job of making it look presentable. Without CSS, we would be awash in blue, underlined hypertext links and default fonts.

CSS works in several ways:

• inline styles that are incorporated into singular HTML items,

• internal stylesheets that apply to one page,

• and external stylesheets that can be applied to multiple pages.

As websites moved towards a more designed presentation, inline styles were very common and were perhaps the best way to style content. For writing single pages, inline styles were great as you can dictate the presentation of each aspect. However, if an element repeats across several pages, you need to edit each instance when making changes to the overall appearance of a website – changing one object does not have a domino effect.

Some less advanced systems, such as HTML email templates, do still use inline styles, so it is useful to familiarise yourself with the way they work. Below is an example of a link styled in this way:

```
<a style="color:red; text-
transform:uppercase;" href="http://www.
nameofsite.com/" target="_blank">Link
text goes here</a>
```

Styling links:
By default, a hyperlink will appear in all browsers according to the following conventions: an unvisited link (a:link) is underlined and blue; a visited link (a:visited) is underlined and purple; and an active link (a:active) is underlined and red.

We will show you below how to customise your link styles to keep consistency with your design and colour scheme.

[See more: Colour for the Web, page 124].

```
a:link, a:visited {
    color: #CC0000;
    text-decoration: underline;
}

a:active, a:hover {
    color: #444444;
    text-decoration: none;
}
```

CSS may be applied to a HTML document one of a three ways, as an inline, internal or external style.

Inline styles
The most old-fashioned (and cumbersome) way of styling an element using CSS is to apply it to the individual HTML tag. This method is still used for many email templates as it is difficult to get them to link to external styles. This way of working is largely disregarded due to the associated workflow issues – if a client wants you to change a body font, you will have to go into every instance and update it, or get really good and find and change commands.

```
<h1 style="color:tomato; font-size:
40px;">This is an example title</h1>
```

Internal styles

Internal styles are generally used for single-page websites. The styles are housed in the HTML document in its head section.

```
<head>
<style>
body {
    background-color: #fff;
    font: Arial, Helvetica,
    sans-serif;
    color: #666;
    font-size: 15px;
}
h1 {
    color: tomato;
    font-size: 40px;
}
h2 {
    color: tomato;
    font-size: 30px;
}
</style>
</head>
```

External styles

For the majority of jobs, external styles are the best way of working. If your site has more than one page, you don't want to waste time tracking changes across documents, and you definitely don't want to edit items using inline styles. An external CSS sheet can be linked to any number of pages, and when you update the rules, all of the attached pages will update automatically. In terms of workflow, consistency and complication, this is by far the best approach.

To achieve this, all you have to do is link to a .css file (in the visual below, it is housed in a folder named CSS) and put a snippet similar to this in the header of each page you would like to link. You could also link to several CSS files should you need to apply very specific styling to a few pages, but the majority follow a basic template.

```
<head>
<link rel="stylesheet" type="text/css"
href="css/styles.css">
</head>
```

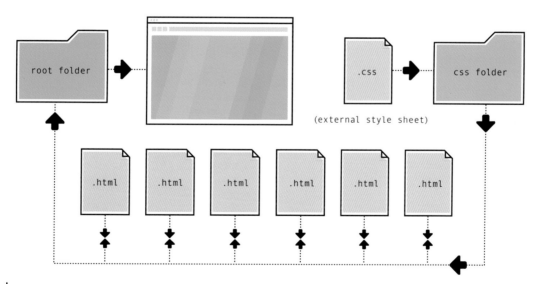

An ideal file structure
All HTML files are housed in a root folder, and the CSS is separated in a subdirectory.

Div id and class

Div is short for division – it allows the developer to circle off a certain amount of content and apply very specific rules. Before the advent of CSS3 and HTML5, it was used to define headers, footers, sidebars and areas of content. Now, HTML5 uses specific semantic tags to define these areas, but div tags are still useful as they allow the developer to treat similar areas of content differently. For example, you may have distinct footer sections, and the HTML5 `<footer>` alone would not be enough to differentiate between them.

There are two types of divs: id and class. An id is more powerful than a class and it is normally used to define large structural areas, whereas a class is used to style and define repeating areas of content.

```
<div id="soups">
  <ol>
    <li>Vegetable</li>
    <li>Broccoli and stilton</li>
    <li>Butternut Squash</li>
    <li>Lentil</li>
  </ol>
</div>

<div class="milkshakes">
  <ul>
    <li>Vanilla</li>
    <li>Strawberry</li>
    <li>Chocolate</li>
    <li>Banana</li>
  </ul>
</div>
```

To refer to these divs in CSS you would create rules much like any others, but you need to refer to the instances in very different ways. A div id is referred to in CSS with a #, the class is referred to with a . (dot) in front of the name of the section. Much like other CSS rules, these can be stacked if they have multiple features in common.

```
#soups, .milkshakes {
   font: Arial, Helvetica,
   sans-serif;
   color: #dedede;
   padding: 10px;
}

#soups {
   background-color: tomato;
}

.milkshakes {
   background-color: pink;
}
```

1. Vegetable
2. Broccoli and stilton
3. Butternut Squash
4. Lentil

- Vanilla
- Strawberry
- Chocolate
- Banana

An example of list types
Top is an ordered list, below is an unordered list.

Positioning elements

One of the greatest uses of CSS beyond styling content is positioning elements on the page in a way that goes beyond the normal 'top-down' flow of a document. There are a few options available in terms of positioning – static, relative, fixed, absolute and sticky.

Static

The static position property is the default; it keeps elements within the normal flow of the document.

```
#soups {
   position: static;
}
```

Fixed

If you want an element to stay in one particular place in the browser window, regardless of scrolling and other content, you might use:

```
#soups {
   position: fixed;
   top: 0px;
   left: 0px;
}
```

Relative

The relative position property is relative to its normal position on the page; therefore, you can play with its top, right, bottom, and left properties.

Since it uses the normal position as a referent, no other elements will flood in.

```
#soups {
   position: relative;
   top: 10px;
   left: 10px;
}
```

Absolute

The absolute position property allows you to position an element relative to its parent (itself, an element relative to the window, or fixed); an element is the parent when it transmits some of its properties to the child that you are positioning.

Therefore, the absolute position property allows you to overlap elements, or to link two elements together in the flow of your web page.

```
#soups {
   position: relative;
   top: 10px;
   left: 10px;
}
#soup-price {
   position: absolute;
   bottom: 30px;
   left: 10px;
   right: 10px;
   display: block;
}
```

Sticky

The sticky position property allows an element to behave as a relative one, following the scroll movements, until it reaches a configured threshold beyond which it behaves as a fixed element, staying in the same place.

```
#soup {
   position: sticky;
   top: 0px;
}
```

[For more examples, see: www.wdgd.co.uk]

Floats

Floats are perhaps one of the most important CSS rules, as they allow you to stack content horizontally as well as vertically. Generally, HTML by default stacks content downwards and, without the float rules, it was very difficult to get content to sit side-by-side. The example below details the method for getting elements to sit at opposite sides of the browser window:

```
#soups {
    background-color: tomato;
    float: left;
    width: 350px;
    height: 350px;
}

#milkshakes {
    background-color: pink;
    float: right;
    width: 350px;
    height: 350px;
}
```

This example will stack the content side by side. By using float: left on both objects, they will move towards the left of the page and stack in the order of your HTML markup. Further objects that utilise the same code will do the same until there is no room left on that row – at this point, they will form another row and continue to stack left along this.

```
#soups {
    background-color: tomato;
    float: left;
    width: 350px;
    height: 350px;
}

#milkshakes {
    background-color: pink;
    float: left;
    width: 350px;
    height: 350px;
}
```

[For more examples, see: www.wdgd.co.uk]

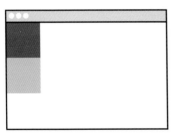

No floats applied

Both objects migrate to the left of the page, stacking from the top-down.

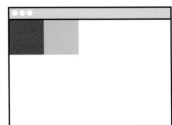

Floats applied, option 1

Soups floated left, and milkshakes floated right.

Floats applied, option 2

When both (or multiple) objects are floated left, they stack side by side.

CSS3

CSS3 builds on previous CSS terminology but adds a number of functions, such as rotate, fade and transform. Any of these rules can be applied directly to an object, or triggered by a rollover.

To make an image fade on rollover, you might use CSS like:

```
img {
  opacity:0.6;
}

img:hover {
  opacity:1;
}
```

Simple effects, such as adding rounded corners to a container are possible using:

```
#milkshakes {
  background-color: pink;
  border-radius: 6px;
  background-clip: padding-box;
  float: left;
  width: 350px;
}
```

(background-clip ensures that there is no overspill into the rounded corners of the container by media contained within)

CSS3 also allows for a much lighter workload when it comes to specifying fonts. With previous CSS incarnations, the designer would specify a font as:

```
p {
  font-family: Georgia, Times, serif;
  font-size: 12px;
  line-height: 16px;
  font-weight: normal;
}
```

However, now the same effect can be achieved with a single line:

```
p {
  font: normal 12px/16px Georgia, Times,
  serif;
}
```

Additionally, a numbers of fonts can be included in your designs with the @font-face rule:

```
@font-face {
  font-family: 'WebFont';
  src: url('font/WebFont.eot');
  src: url('font/WebFont.eot?#iefix')
  format('embedded-opentype'),
  url('font/WebFont.woff2')
  format('woff2'),
  url('font/WebFont.woff')
  format('woff'),
  url('font/WebFont.ttf')
  format('truetype'),
  url('font/WebFont.svg#WebFont')
  format('svg');
}
```

The above CSS will look for the various font files in a folder named 'fonts'. A number of font files are required, as certain file types work better on different devices and computers.

[For more examples, see: www.wdgd.co.uk]

PHP

PHP, or Hypertext Preprocessor can be combined with HTML and CSS to provide greater functionality, allowing you to control files on the server and update your database.

It is commonly used in Content Management Systems (such as Drupal, Joomla and WordPress) as it allows for separation of the content from the markup – a client can use a WYSIWYG editor to add content to an SQL database, and PHP will then query this and present the information in the relevant pages you have designed.

Beyond this, PHP also has simpler uses such as creating contact forms. One really simple application is to fetch the current year and update your copyright information in the footer of your site. You can achieve this with the following:

```
<p> My Example Site &copy; <?php echo
date("Y"); ?> </p>
```

SQL

SQL (or Structured Query Language) is a database system and set of tools that exists server-side and stores information that can be added to, and manipulated by users with the correct access privileges.

The database is made up of tables that contain relational data stored in fields and can be cross-referenced by a search. A developer can utilise PHP (or similar) to query the database, select specific information, and then display this using HTML and CSS.

For example, if we were to create a table called 'MailList' with SQL to store mailing list information, it may look like this:

ID	First name	Surname	Email	Country
1	Fiona	Park	fpark@example.com	UK
2	Alan	Bouvet	abouvet@example.com	USA
3	Max	Power	mpower@example.com	India
4	Terry	Phillips	tphillips@example.com	Australia
5	Mary	Dorough	mdorough@example.com	Ireland

Each row of the table contains a number of records for each customer, and this can be queried as such if you wish to retrieve all information:

```
SELECT * FROM MailList;
```

However, if you only want to select email addresses, you could use as your query:

```
SELECT Email FROM MailList;
```

JavaScript

HTML deals with the content of a page, and CSS defines the presentation; JavaScript looks after the behaviour. It can be used to create sophisticated interactions and simple rollover effects. One very basic example is the creation of a button that allows users to close a browser window (especially useful if you are using pop-ups):

```
<button onclick="closeWin()">Close "my-
Window"</button>
```

JavaScript works by targeting elements on the page (with the getElementById function), listening for user events (such as mouseover or onclick), by citing variables and functions, and many other methods. JavaScript uses this input to trigger interactions or update content on the page.

The following example will populate the <p> tags with flavours of milkshakes. It achieves this as the empty <p> tags are assigned unique IDs that correspond with the values assigned by the variables in the script section. This example can be included in the body of your HTML document.

```
<h2>Milkshakes</h2>
<p id="flavour"> </p>
<p id="flavour2"> </p>

<script>
var Milkshakes = "Vanilla";
document.getElementById("flavour").
innerHTML = Milkshakes;
var Milkshakes = "Strawberry";
document.getElementById("flavour2").
innerHTML = Milkshakes;
</script>
```

This example will allow the user to switch between images with the click of a button:

```
<img src="img/image1.jpg" id="demo">

<button type="button"
onclick="myFunction()">Try it</button>

<script>
function myFunction() {
    document.getElementById("demo").
    src='img/image2.jpg';
}
</script>
```

The image is assigned a unique ID of "demo" and the button is assigned the function "myFunction". Once the button is clicked, it will look for the relevant function and ID and then swap the image for the one detailed in the script. Again, this can be placed anywhere within your website's body.

JQuery

JQuery is a lightweight central repository of JavaScripts that the developer will link to in order to trigger a number of functions. Common JQuery functions include lightbox effects, accordion and dropdown menus, scrolling galleries and media controllers. To get JQuery running on your page you simply link to the latest version in your head tags and then call functions when required in the main body of your page. It is best to store the JQuery version on your server alongside your HTML and CSS documents – many developers create a directory (foler) named 'JS' to store these files.

```
<head>
<script src="js/jquery-3.1.1.min.js"></
script>
</head>
```

A simple JQuery example is the 'spoiler' – a button that shows and hides content. To achieve this effect, you need to place the following functions in your header. Within the document, the query will search for a div ID called 'spoiler' (this is the target – the object that will be affected). It will also search for two objects (in this case buttons) called #show and #hide. The function at the top that is not looking for a 'click' is there to ensure no content is visible as the page loads – #spoiler loads hidden.

```
<script>
$(document).ready(function(){
        $("#spolier").hide();
    });
$(document).ready(function(){
    $("#hide").click(function(){
        $("#spolier").hide();
    });
    $("#show").click(function(){
        $("#spolier").show();
    });
});
</script>
```

This next snippet goes in the body of your page and is the range of objects the query is looking for.

```
<h2>Spoiler alert!</h2>

<button id="show">Show</button>
<button id="hide">Hide</button>

<div id="spolier">
<p>Some content.</p>
<p>Some more content.</p>
</div>
```

The simple .hide and .show function in the script will now mask the spoiler content.

[For more examples, see: www.wdgd.co.uk]

Cookies

Cookies are small amounts of data downloaded to your browser when you visit a website. The data documents may include such information as whether you've been to the page before, login details, whether items have been added to your shopping cart, and more. Although cookies speed up browsing, this type of tracking does bring about privacy concerns. Due to these concerns, developers are now required to make users aware that cookies are being downloaded and users have to offer informed consent.

Cookies and consent
It is vital that all websites carry clear information regarding the use of visitors' data, and that visitors give consent for their data to be used.

Advanced coding

There are many other types of coding languages that can be used across websites and apps. Commonly used examples of high-level programing languages in active use today include Processing, C++, Python, Perl, PHP, ECMAScript, Ruby, Visual Basic, Delphi and more.

Processing was developed by Ben Fry and Casey Reas. It is an open source platform that builds on Java and allows the designer to create data visualisations, animations, games and interactive visual arts pieces. Processing.js allows Processing code to be run in the browser

C++ (Derived from C) is a multipurpose coding language that can be used in websites, applications and within a number of contexts. Commonly within website design, this language is used for search engines, e-commerce and is the basis of some social media platforms. However, C++ is not known for its speed, and therefore,

several other languages went on to become more popular.

Python is a widely-used general-purpose programing language and a much more streamlined one than C++. Developed in the 1980s, Python can also be used to develop desktop and browser-specific applications. Many large websites, such as Google and Wikipedia, use Python for certain functions.

Ruby is used as a web application framework, and from this, Ruby on Rails was developed to provide database functionality on websites that support e-commerce and user-based environments.

Pearl (Practical Extraction and Reporting Language) is widely used on the Web as a CGI (Common Gateway Interface) tool – this allows the user to input data and the CGI converts this into HTML.

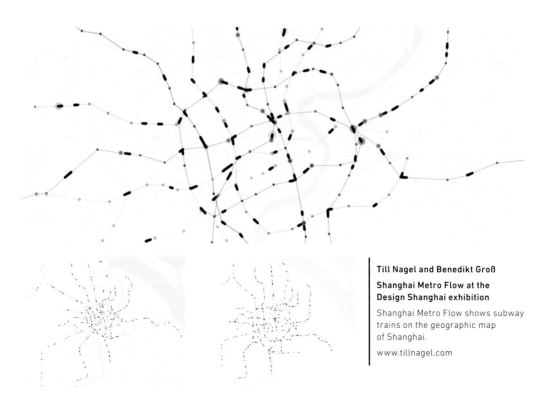

Till Nagel and Benedikt Groß

Shanghai Metro Flow at the Design Shanghai exhibition

Shanghai Metro Flow shows subway trains on the geographic map of Shanghai.

www.tillnagel.com

In terms of developing apps, SDKs (Software Development Kits) are a set of development tools that are typically specific to certain platforms. Android applications require an SDK with Java; iOS (Apple) apps employ an iOS SDK with Swift, and MS Windows utilises the .NET Framework SDK with .NET.

Xcode is an environment created for developing software for macOS, iOS, watchOS and tvOS. It utilises a range of programming languages; Android employs a similar Developer Lab and this includes Bootcamps to get developers started.

In addition to app development, there are also microcontrollers: small single integrated circuit computers that contains basic processor cores, a small amount of memory and programmable inputs and outputs. These tools are used often to control the 'internet of things' and you may find them in washing machines, hair dryers, telephones, and anything with an LED/LCD screen, sensor and/or a keyboard. This technology doesn't just allow machines to be programmed individually, but also linked through an internet connection. Because of these devices, more

and more everyday household objects can be programmed and controlled remotely.

An Arduino is an open-source single-board microcontroller that is used across a wide range of projects due to its versatility. With the Arduino, you can create controllers for devices, generative systems, and functions that respond to external inputs such as heat and light.

The Raspberry Pi is a single-board computer developed in the UK by the Raspberry Pi Foundation, and it is used to teach school children basic programming. It is very low cost, and later models come equipped with Bluetooth, WiFi and USB capabilities. Similar to the Arduino, it can be used to control other devices and respond to external inputs. Users have gone as far as to creating microwaves, game consoles and mobile phones with this platform.

The We-io that allows for programs to built using simple HTML5, JavaScript and Python. With this you can connect objects and make applications that drive motors, sensors, lights and more, all through an associated web browser.

Till Nagel and Benedikt Groß
Shanghai Metro Flow at the Design Shanghai exhibition
Transitions between geographical and schematic maps show how different representations of the city have very distinct characteristics. Visualizing the distortion of inner and outer urban areas illustrates how maps not only transform the image of the city, but also influence our perception of space. This piece is created with processing.
www.tillnagel.com

Processing

Processing and its spin-offs – such as P5.js, Processing.js and Processing.py – are used by artists and designers for offline and online interactive and/or generative artefacts. They offer a new approach to programming.

You can download Processing from: https://processing.org/

In this section, you can find some basic Processing principles and features that will facilitate your first piece of programming (also called 'sketch'). Please note that Processing is 'case sensitive' – you should pay attention to your use of lower and upper cases when calling a function and naming or using your variables.

[For the files, see: www.wdgd.co.uk]

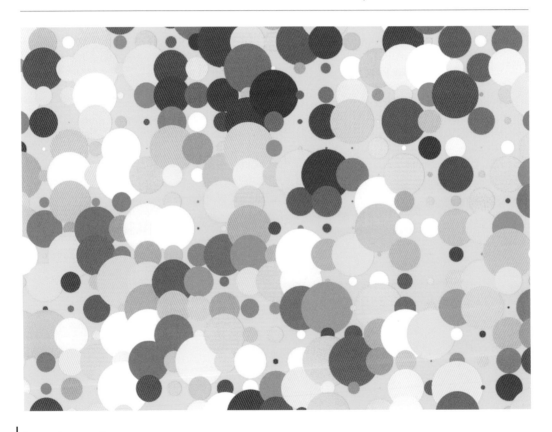

Processing example

Through pages 103 to 110, you will learn how to create a piece of generative design using processing.

You can find more information about the background here:

www.processing.org/reference/background_.html

And you can find more information about the RGB mode here:

www.w3schools.com/colors/colors_rgb.asp

Processing basics

Processing is used by graphic designers to create generative designs. In generative design, the designer first creates a set of parameters for the shape, the colour and the position of the graphical elements. Processing uses an algorithm to randomly render these graphic elements, creating unique images or short animations. This chapter will show you the basics that will allow you to set up the parameters to generate your design.

Step 1a – The stage or canvas
//this is size of your playground in pixels
```
size(500, 500);
```

//your canvas colour background in RGB
```
background(255,255,0);
```

Step 2a – How to draw a shape (rectangle)
The function 'rect' defines the type of shape you want to draw, the numbers are respectively for the x (the horizontal position of your rectangle left top corner), the y (the vertical position of your rectangle left top corner), the width and the height of your rectangle.

In other words, you're telling Processing first to select a shape that is a rectangle – rect – , then you're telling it where on the playground to place this shape – x and y – then you specify the dimensions of your shape – height and width.

//shape type, x, y, width, height
```
rect(20,25,50,60);
```

Without specifications, your shape should have a white fill and a black stroke.

Step 2b – How to change the colour of my shape

//fill my shape with a RGB color, a bright red
```
fill(255,0,0);
```
//remove the stroke
```
noStroke();
```

Step 3 – How to draw an ellipse
```
fill(0,25,255);
stroke(0,0,200);
ellipse(100,50,80,80);
```

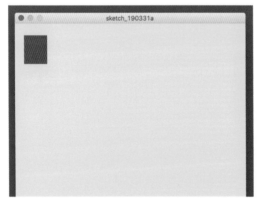

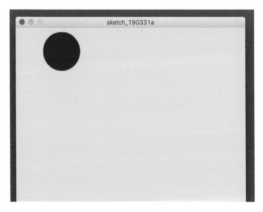

Please note that in your sketch you should specify the filling and stroke nature before drawing your rectangle.

Step 4 – How to draw a triangle

```
triangle(30, 75, 58, 20, 86, 75);
```

Step 5 – How to draw a line

```
//color of my line stroke
stroke(155);
//my line (x1, y1, x2, y2)
line(100, 75, 200, 75);
```

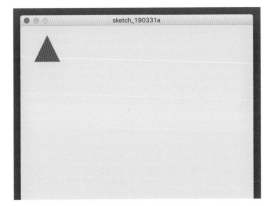

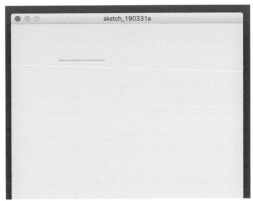

Please note that if you have not specified the fill and the stroke nature of your third shape, it is going to refer to the last specified features. In other words, if you do not use the fill() and stroke() functions just before calling the triangle function, then your triangle will have the same fill and stroke as your ellipse, higher in the code lines.

Step 6a – What is the 'random' function?
The 'random' function generates random numbers; it means that each time the function is called, it will return an unexpected value within a specified range. In other words, if you want to obtain a number between 0 and 9, you will write:

//random(high)
```
Random(10);
```

Please note that Processing will pick up a number from a stack of ten, as specified, but since it starts counting from 0, the possible results are as following: 0, 1, 2, 3, 4, 5, 6, 7, 8 and 9.

If you want to have a result between 1 and 10, you will have to write:

//random(low, high)
```
Random(1, 10);
```

Step 6b – How to use the 'random' function
We are going to use the same code as the previous steps but with a few modifications in red:

//size of your playground in pixels
```
size(500, 500);
```

//canvas colour background in RGB
```
background(255,255,0); //bright yellow
```

//fill my following shape with a RGB color
```
fill(255,0,0);
```

//remove the stroke of my following shape
```
noStroke();
```

//shape type, x, y, width, height
```
rect(random(5,375),25,50,60);
```

// here, we have replaced a 'static' number with a function that is re-actualised each time the sketch is launched.

//my ellipse
```
fill(0,25,255);
stroke(0,0,200);
ellipse(300,200,200,200);
```

//my triangle
```
triangle(30, 75, 58, 20, 86, 75);
```

//my line
//color of my line stroke
```
stroke(155);
```

//my line (x1, y1, x2, y2)
```
line(100, 75, 200, 75);
```

Each time you launch your sketch, the position of your rectangle has changed. You can play with the function and try to change any number by it to see the result (shape and colours).

Step 7a – The 'loop' function

The 'loop' function allows you to draw a series of shapes without repeating the same code lines several times.

'i' and 'j' are two variables whose names have been chosen arbitrarily, but programmers use them by conventions; they are the John and Jane Doe of programming. They will allow us to store the temporary result of the incrementation (+ +) and apply it to each iteration of your shape. The 'i' value is for the horizontal positions of your ellipses, while the 'j' is for their vertical positions.

For each 'i' starting from zero and finishing at fifty, the value of 'i' will be incremented by two (the '+ +').

```
fill(0,25,255);
```

```
//define the constraints of your 50 ellipses
horizontal positions
for(int i=0;i<50;i++){
```

```
//define the constraints of your 50 ellipses
vertical positions
for(int j=0;j<50;j++){
```

```
//then draw the ellipse (x,y, width, height)
   ellipse(i*10,j*10, 2, 2);
   }
}
```

Step 7b – How to use the 'loop' function with the 'random' function

Once you are familiar with the principle of the loop, you can start combining it with other functions such as the 'random' one:

```
//size of your playground in pixels
size(500, 500);
background(255,255,0);
```

```
//fill my following shape with a RGB color
fill(255,0,0);
```

```
//remove the stroke of my following shape
noStroke();
```

```
//shape type, x, y, width, height
rect(random(5,375),25,50,60);
```

```
//my random ellipse
for(int i=0; i<50;i++){
   for(int j=0; j<50;j++){
      fill(random(200,255),
      random(50,150),200);
      float diameter = random(1,10);
      ellipse(i*10, j*10, diameter,
      diameter);
   }
}
```

```
//my triangle
triangle(30, 75, 58, 20, 86, 75);
```

```
//my line
//color of my line stroke
stroke(155);
```

```
//my line (x1, y1, x2, y2)
line(100, 75, 200, 75);
```

107

Until now you have been working within the 'static' mode of Processing; everything you code is drawn once and for all. In the next section, we will see how to program within the 'active' mode in order to add some interactivity to your sketch.

Step 1a – Set up your 'active' mode
All you have to do is to add the 'set up' function at the beginning of your line of code, and to close the same function with a '}' before calling the 'draw' function. The 'set up' function is just called one, when your sketch is launched.

```
void setup() {

//size of your playground in pixels
size(500, 500);
}
```

You can then call the 'draw' function and this will execute the code below:

Step 1b – Add the 'draw' function
```
//The draw function is called
void draw() {

//canvas colour background in RGB
background(255,255,0);

//fill my following shape with a RGB color
fill(255,0,0);

//remove the stroke of my following shape
noStroke();

//shape type, x, y, width, height

rect(20,25,50,60);
```

```
//my random ellipse
for(int i=0; i<50;i++){
   for(int j=0; j<50;j++){
      fill(random(200,255),
      random(50,150),200);
      float diameter = random(1,10);
      ellipse(i*10, j*10, diameter,
      diameter);
   }
 }


//my triangle
triangle(30, 75, 58, 20, 86, 75);


//my line
//color of my line stroke
stroke(155);


//my line (x1, y1, x2, y2)
line(100, 75, 200, 75);
 }


//do not forget to close your function with
the bracket.
```

Feel free to play with the variables: the colours, the number, the shapes and the positions of the ellipses and try to apply the 'loop' and 'random' functions to your triangles and rectangles. Once you are happy, you can export the result into a pdf.

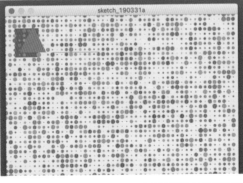

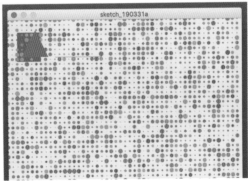

Export your image in .pdf

To export your result in pdf, first, you have to tell Processing that you will need a specific function called 'processing.pdf'. This function is not installed by default in Processing because of its weight and should be called only when it is used, therefore, the function processing.pdf is stored in a library that you will import into your sketch: go to the very top horizontal menu of Processing and click on the 'Sketch' drop-down menu, then select 'import library > pdf'.

Once you have imported your library, Processing adds this line to your code at the very beginning of your sketch – before the set up function:

```
import processing.pdf.*;

void setup() {
```

```
//for a A4 in 300 dpi, the scene
dimensions should be as follow:
size(2480, 3508);
noLoop();
```

```
//Save my image "MyImage" and to add
a timestamp in the filename to make in unique.
It will save in the same folder as your
Processing sketch.
beginRecord(PDF, "MyImage"+ year()+mon
th()+day()+hour()+minute()+second()+".
pdf");
}
void draw() {
```

```
//canvas colour background in RGB
background(255,255,0);
```

```
//the variable height is the height of my scene
declared in the set up
//my ellipses
//remove the stroke of my following shape
noStroke();
```

```
for(int i=0; i<50;i++){
for(int j=0; j<50;j++){
fill(random(200,255), random(50,150),200);
float diameter = random(10,200);
ellipse(i*(width/50), j*(height/50),
diameter, diameter);
}
}
endRecord();
}
```

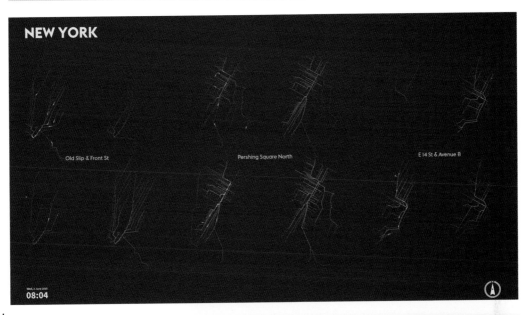

**Till Nagel and Christopher Pietsch,
Urban Complexity Lab, FH Potsdam**

**City flows Citywide view
of New York City**

Below is an installation with
an interactive column controlling three
screens showing bike trajectories
in New York City, Berlin, and London.
This piece is created with processing.

www.tillnagel.com

www.uclab.fh-potsdam.de/cf/

Meet the designers: What is your educational background?

Inayaili de León

In high school, I studied arts, because that was the path you needed
to take if you wanted to be an architect (which I did). But a few weeks before
university applications, I decided to study design instead, so I have a degree
in communications design.

Bruce Lawson

I'm an English Literature and Drama graduate, who then went into programing
as a graduate trainee, then trained as an English teacher to go travelling.

Dan Hinton

From an early age I knew I wanted to do something within the design world.
Straight out of school I studied a BTEC in graphic design at college. Following
this I went to the Arts University Bournemouth to study a two-year foundation
degree in Visual Communication. I then went on to top this up, coming away
with a BA Hons in Graphic Design.

Ricky Gane

I have studied to A-level standard, but the majority of my training was on the
job. I think this has given me a drive and desire to constantly progress, learn
and push myself, and it gives me a different perspective than the traditional
education route would have given me.

Sush Kelly

I went to Uni to study Visual Communication and ended up specialising
in Illustration. Upon graduating I quickly realised my illustrative style had too
many 'fangs' and wasn't commercial enough. My interest in the Web grew as I
built my own site to try and get work. I had a chance meeting with someone
at the Job Centre, and it turned out her boyfriend worked for a design agency
and they needed a designer. Despite my illustration heavy portfolio they must
have seen something in me as I got the gig.

Sylvie Daumal

Literature and Design, but it was a very long time ago... I feel that I have been shaped in a more significant way by my professional experiences during the last fifteen years.

Ross Chapman

School, college and a University degree is how I got started, but I'm a life-long learner. I don't binge watch Game of Thrones, or play computer games on my evenings and weekends. What I tend to do is use Google to find out what I need to learn and then go ahead and execute. For me, confidence just comes from practice, whether that be facilitating a workshop, designing an app or doing a talk, but for finding ideas, the Internet or a few choice books have helped me out in the past.

Nodesign

Architecture and Industrial Design degrees from the best schools in Europe.

Amy Parker

I have a Bachelor of Science degree in Media Arts and Design from Northeastern University.

Jamie Homer

My path started with A-Level Art. From there I had to enrol onto what was called an access course, which essentially gave you access to a whole lot of other routes through education. This was a one year ND foundation course, where I was able to specialise in graphic design. Following that, I went to college at Taunton's fabulous Somerset College of Art and Design where I completed an HND in graphic design followed by a degree in graphic design.

CHAPTER 4:
DESIGNING FOR THE WEB AND PLATFORMS

As a graphic designer approaching a web design project, you already know a great deal of the information required to undertake the brief. Every brief you've undertaken has an audience, a client and hopefully a solution that pleases both.

You will have formed a visual and textual piece that employs various visual communication/composition skills and relies on a considered, well-researched approach – ways of adapting and utilising this knowledge is covered in the first half of this chapter.

In many ways, designing for the Web is not so different from a publishing project, but there are a few more aspects you will need to consider. These are covered in the latter parts of this chapter and through the next sections of this book.

Planning your designs – from paper to the screen

Once you have a clear idea who your customer is, start designing with paper and pencil. Thumbnailing will help you work out proportions and scale – it's quicker than using Photoshop or coding a page, and drawings will quickly highlight problems. You can also use gridded paper to work out the exact proportions of your underlying grid, typographic hierarchies and proportions of image to text. Use paper to work out the flow of your website and the levels of navigation.

A sitemap is incredibly important as you need to know how many page templates you will need to design, how these will flow and exactly what types of content you are designing for. Determine page types (portfolio pages, landing page, contact, blog articles, etc.) and consider what systems these pages will follow (normally headers and footers stay consistent across a website), and then start designing the unique elements.

Once you have a plan for the design, start with mock-ups and wireframing. Wireframes are simple designs that usually employ dummy content but work in the browser. With these, you will start to see how your designs fare on different browser ratios and devices.

Perhaps, most importantly, forget Photoshop and learn to prototype with code. If you can develop this skill, you will have HTML-ready designs that you can improve on, rather than PSD files that won't give the client a true feel for usability in the browser.

Sitemaps

Image above and over: The sitemap and wireframe stage of a student's interactive application project.

Photography credit: Andrew Way and Alexander Lucas

Visual communication for the Web and digital platforms

Communication on the Web is in many ways similar to print design – largely, you will be dealing with image and text. However, alongside these key elements, you will also encounter various types of interactivity (buttons, for example), video, sound, animation and more.

Again, similar to print, you will need to establish a set of rules that will guide your designs and create a uniformity and consistency. Whereas InDesign employs paragraph styles, websites use Cascading Style Sheets [for more, see: CSS, page 90] to ensure consistency. Websites will also use grid systems [for more see: Grids, page 150] to help the designer plot the page.

Unlike print, you have several levels of interaction that you need to contend with, and you need to guide the user through these systems. There are many established systems that will be familiar to many web users, such as underlining links and making them a different colour to the body copy.

Icons such as the hamburger menu and home icon are familiar to many, but do not feel you need to follow exactly what others are doing. As long as you can establish a clear visual system that users understand, the site should be easily navigated.

Also, don't feel that consistency means boring, plain design. You can challenge viewers as long as you don't confuse them. Try to avoid systems that are too conventional like sticking to 100 per cent black text on a 100 per cent white background; and even though the work is destined for the screen, you can use texture.

Visual research

So, where do you start researching? The simple (and scary) answer is everywhere!

For some inexperienced digital designers, there is a tendency to forget everything they know about print design when they approach a website. All of the same rules apply as with any other creative project – you are still dealing with text and image, issues of legibility and communication.

As with any other graphic design project, you need to understand the needs of the audience. Observe people to see how they interact with technology and web pages. Conduct surveys, hold round-table discussions, test your ideas and most importantly, listen to the end-user.

Look at the design people (or more specifically, your intended audience) you encounter on a daily basis. Research fashion for colours, pattern, etc. Look to graphic design for layout, typography, hierarchy, etc. The brand the end-users encounter through their everyday lives will give you some clue as to their visual expectations. You will need to know your audience's spending power, their gender, their lifestyle, and much more.

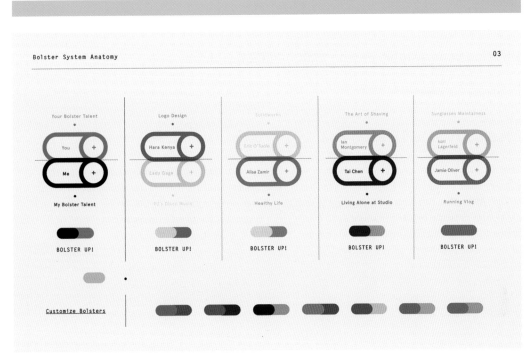

Tai Chen

Bolsters (images this page and over)

Bolsters is a system that connects people at different life stages. These images show the development of the project including colour and typeface choice, layout experiments, and eventual designs. Tai has established a clear visual system that is consistent, colour and visually striking.

www.behance.net/ChenHueiTai

Utilising your graphic design skills and knowledge

Designing for the screen isn't a million miles away from designing for print. While the context may be quite different (and you do have a few different considerations), it is still a visual medium.

There are many areas of commonality; these include basic design principles such as scale, colour, hierarchy, proportion, typography, etc. Most web projects will have similar structural elements to those encountered in a magazine or book design project, as you will need

to consider titles, body copy, boxouts, the relationship between the text and image, etc. The process for rendering these might be less familiar, but you know how to handle them.

As web technologies have advanced, it has become much easier to render outcomes that are more in line with print projects – you have a greater range of colours to play with, and access to a greater range of typefaces.

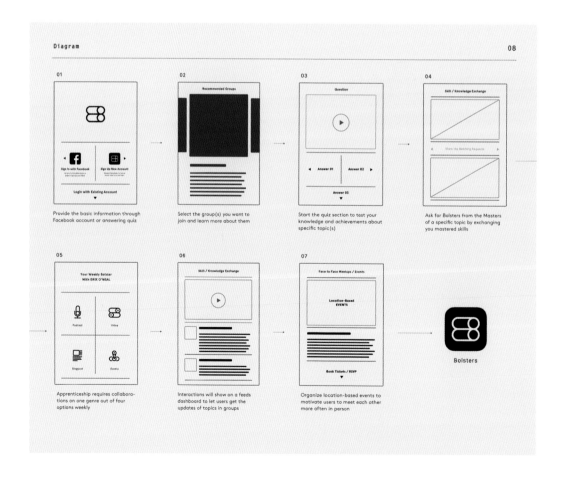

Diagram · 08

01 Provide the basic information through Facebook account or answering quiz

02 Select the group(s) you want to join and learn more about them

03 Start the quiz section to test your knowledge and achievements about specific topic(s)

04 Ask for Bolsters from the Masters of a specific topic by exchanging you mastered skills

05 Apprenticeship requires collaborations on one genre out of four options weekly

06 Interactions will show on a feeds dashboard to let users get the updates of topics in groups

07 Organize location-based events to motivate users to meet each other more often in person

Bolsters

ꝊꝊ   EVENT LIST: THE NOTE OF BILL EVANS   • • •

Schedule Up Your Visits With The Bolsters: JUSTIN ANDERSON

<u>2018.06. 05</u> <u>Showtime: 8:00PM</u> <u>Doors Open at 6:00PM</u>

Ticket / RSVP   <u>TicketMaster.com</u>

Contact   <u>Bluenote.net</u> | <u>702 292 6543</u>
                  <u>131 W 3rd St, New York, NY 10012</u>

More Information

◄

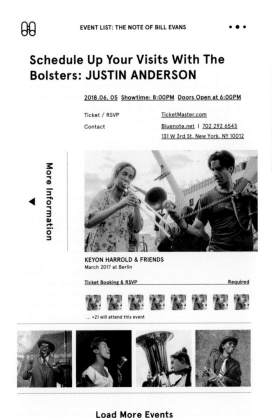

KEYON HARROLD & FRIENDS
March 2017 at Berlin

Ticket Booking & RSVP   Required

... +21 will attend this event

Load More Events
▼

< EVENT: JUSTIN ANDERSON AT BLUE NOTE   • • •

Discover The Blue Note NYC with JUSTIN ANDERSON

<u>EriK O'Neal</u> & <u>Davie Burgson</u> orgnized this activity for the members from **The Note of Bill Evans**, but feel free to invite all your friends to join the event.

Cited by Wynton Marsalis as the "future of the trumpet" and "one of the most sought after trumpeters in the world", this St. Louis native and Mannes School of Music graduate is an eclectic trumpeter/music producer/arranger/songwriter who is known for pushing musical boundaries through his compositions and improvisational style.

As a go-to trumpeter in the music industry having been featured on nearly 100 albums ranging from jazz, R&B, pop, gospel, blues and hip hop, Harrold has toured and recorded with or produced for some of the world's best artists and ensembles. Such artists include Jay-Z, Beyoncé, Common, Erykah Badu, Lauryn Hill, Mary J Blige, Rihanna, Gregory Porter, Andre Crouch, David Sanborn, D'Angelo and the Vanguard, Billy Harper, Robert Glasper, 50 Cent, and LL Cool J, to name a few. In particular, he is an integral part of two-time Grammy-Award winning album "Black Summer's Night" by R&B icon Maxwell with whom he has had a long collaboration having arranged, composed and produced various songs. He also has had numerous musical placements in film and TV including the upcoming Miles Davis Biopic "Miles Ahead" directed by Don Cheadle (film score by Robert Glasper) where he is featured as the trumpet sound of Don Cheadle playing Miles Davis. His next album will be released in early 2016.

Book Tickets / RSVP
▼

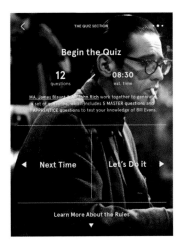

THE QUIZ SECTION

Begin the Quiz

12   08:30
questions   est. time

MA, James Blaunt and John Rich work together to generate a set of questions, which includes 5 MASTER questions and 9 APPRENTICE questions to test your knowledge of Bill Evans.

◄ Next Time   Let's Do it ►

Learn More About the Rules
▼

< THE QUIZ SECTION   • • •

05   ▨▨▨▨☐☐☐☐☐☐☐☐   12

0:32   1:32

◄× ⏮ ⏸ ⏭ ☆

◄ Alice In The Wonderland   Gloria's Step– Take 2 ►

< THE QUIZ SECTION   • • •

08 / 12

                    10 Points to Pass

• • • • • • • ○ • •

You need <u>2 more points</u> to pass this quiz!

◄ **Wait for Next Quiz** 40 Minutes Later   **Ask for Mentoring** from Master List ►

Colour for the Web

When designing for print you will likely use a CMYK mix for your colours, or in certain cases when you need to match a colour exactly, a Pantone colour. CMYK is a subtractive colour model – the absence of ink results in white, and full application of all four colours will lead to black.

When working on projects that are screen-based (using projected light) you will need to use the RGB (red, green and blue) model. This way of mixing colour is additive – when no light is projected you have black, but when you project all three colours equally, you will get white.

RGB
The pairings of digits refer to the amount of red, green and blue in this particular colour mix.

(255,99,71)

RGBA
The first three sets of numbers again refer to the red, green and blue mix while the last digits (0.6 in this case) refers to the opacity of the colour.

(255,99,71,0.6)

Hexadecimal colour values
Again, the pairings of digits refer to the amount of red, green and blue in this particular colour mix. Here, the paired digits are FF, 63 and 47.

#FF6347

Note: some hex colours can be written in a simpler way if the pairings of digits are the same. Pairings such as #FFFFFF or #666666 may be written as #FFF or #666.

HTML Colour names
There is a range of colour values that can be referred to by name. In your CSS file you can specify any of the following to get white:

```
color: #FFF
```

```
color: #FFFFFF
```

```
color: rgb(255,255,255)
```

```
color: rgb(255,255,255,1.0)
```

-or simply:

```
color: white
```

The colour example used throughout this section might also be referred to in your code as tomato.

```
tomato
#ff6347
rgb(255,99,71)
```

Web colour

Above, and over: Examples of web colours, displayed with their web colour name, hexadecimal reference and RGB value. These colours have been converted into CMYK for print, so may not be exact matches of the screen colour.

white
#ffffff
rgb(255,255,255)

black
#000000
rgb(0,0,0)

grey
#808080
rgb(128,128,128)

red
#FF0000
rgb(255,0,0)

green
#008000
rgb(0,128,0)

blue
#0000FF
RGB(0,0,255)

cyan
#00FFFF
RGB(0,255,255)

magenta
#FF00FF
RGB(255,0,255)

yellow
#FFFF00
RGB(255,255,0)

navy
#000080
rgb(0,0,128)

seagreen
#2E8B57
rgb(46,139,87)

purple
#800080
RGB(128,0,128)

indigo
#4B0082
RGB(75,0,130)

lime
#00FF00
RGB(0,255,0)

deeppink
#FF1493
RGB(255,20,147)

lavender
#E6E6FA
RGB(230,230,250)

cornsilk
#FFF8DC
RGB(255, 248, 220)

mintcream
#F5FFFA
RGB(245, 255, 250)

Typography

The first thing most designers do when they start a print project is to override the default settings of a program and create their own rules for the typographic elements – working on web projects should be no different. Each browser comes with its own particular set of defaults and ways of handling headers, body copy, bold words, italics, and more. The styling attached to text-based hyperlinks is different to print projects..

Overall, the rules for handling typography on the Web are similar to print, but with a printed artefact, you will likely design to a fixed and predetermined size. By contrast, an online composition will be viewed on a myriad of browsers, devices, and screen resolutions, all of which require attention and a clear set of rules.

Font stack

You can't know what fonts are installed on the computer of the end-user. If you design a layout with a specific font that is missing from the host machine, then a default font will replace it, and this will probably not work with your design. To avoid this kind of design accident, you can create a font stack based on web-safe fonts. A font stack is a range of similar fonts (pre-installed in each browser) listed within the CSS font-family declaration in order of preference.

In the following example, you ask the browser to first look for and display Helvetica; if Helvetica is not available on the host's computer, then you will ask it to display Arial, or at least a font belonging to the sans-serif family.

```
p {
  font-family: Helvetica, Arial, sans-
  serif;
}
```

Measurements

CSS allows the use of different units to measure the size of the fonts. Some of them come from the paper-based typographic tradition, such as the point (pt), while others are specially created to fit the screen display features, such as the pixel (px) and the em.

By default, web measurement units follow this conversion rule:

1em = 12pt = 16px = 100%.

Measurement in px

Pixels (px) are relative to the viewing device (also called viewport). On early computers and low-dpi devices, 1px is one device pixel of the display. However, for high-resolution monitors and screens, 1px as a unit is, in fact, multiple device pixels.

Other relative common measurement units are em and %. There also new units such as wv (1% of viewport width) and wh (1% of viewport height) that are relative to the size of the application window and are ways of achieving responsive designs.

```
p {
  font-size: 16px;
  font-family: Helvetica, Arial, sans-
  serif;
}
```

Measurement in points

As a graphic designer, you may be tempted to use units that you know well, especially points, as these are standard across most desktop publishing applications. However, pt is an absolute unit that won't allow re-scaling.

124

It could work well on a large screen but could be difficult to read on a smaller device.

```
p {
    font-size: 14pt;
    font-family: Helvetica, Arial, sans-
    serif;
}
```

Measurement in em
The em unit is relative to the font-size of the element or the page. By default, it is 16px, and em allows the end-user to resize the text via the browser menu.

```
p {
    font-size: 1em;
    font-family: Helvetica, Arial, Sans-
    serif;
}
```

Measurement as a percentage
The % unit works like the em but it is relative only to the font size of a parent element.

```
p {
    font-size: 100%;
    font-family: Helvetica, Arial, sans-
    serif;
}
```

Further style options
The size of the font is not the only property you can play with in web typography; you can change the line space (line height), the weight of the font and its style (normal, italic, oblique), add some text decoration (overline, underline, line-through), or propose some small-caps variants.

As we have seen, there are several options for specifying the font-size; similarly, there are several ways to determine the line height. In the following example, 1.6 is a relative unit that will keep the space between lines 1.6 times bigger than the text, whatever the size of the text.

```
p {
    font-size: 14pt;
    line-height: 1.6;
    color: #ccc;
    font-weight: bold;
    font-weight: 700;
    font-style: italic;
    font-variant: small-caps;
}
```

CSS font property
The CSS font property allows you to stack several styling options in one declaration. Rather than separating font size, line height and other options across several lines in your CSS, the following example shows how these can be declared together.

```
p {
    font: bold italic 14pt/1.6
    Helvetica, Arial, sans-serif;
    font-weight: bold;
    font-weight: 700;
    font-style: italic;
}
```

[For more examples, see: www.wdgd.co.uk]

Web fonts

In the very early days of the Web, typography was not a consideration in terms of presenting textual content. Computers had limited fonts available, and the browser used the default. As computers developed, a (limited) set of fonts became the default choices across PCs and Macs, and web browsers began to utilise these typefaces. This new default set included:

Times New Roman

Arial

Helvetica

Trebuchet

Georgia

Verdana

Tahoma

Courier

If a designer wanted to use different fonts, they would have to create an image of the text. This approach was no good for search engines as they need to read editable text and cannot intelligently pick words out of a jpeg file. Furthermore, images are heavy and will slow down the display of the page.

To combat this limited choice (and bad practice), several methods were created to allow designers more options when delivering web projects. The following text highlights some examples of the most common resources used by developers.

Google Fonts

You will not find system fonts on Google, but they offer a range of typefaces that work really well on web platforms as they are designed with this use in mind. It's easy to link to the font files by adding a Java snippet to your page headers, or you can link to the files in your CSS document.

```
@import url(http://fonts.googleapis.com/
css?family=Open+Sans);
```

```
body {
    font-family: 'Open Sans', sans-serif;
}
```

Font Squirrel

If you have a typeface that you own the full Web rights to, or have created your own font file, a Web font can be created using Font Squirrel. The generator will create a number of files that work on different devices, and you can call the fonts through your CSS with the tag @font-face. The site also houses a number of fonts already equipped with web-ready files that you can download and use for free, or at very little cost.

Once converted, you can add it in your .css by creating a rule in your CSS like the following, declaring the path to the source of this font with:

```
src: url
```

```
@font-face {
font-family: 'myfontname'; src:
url('mywebfont.woff') format('woff');
}
```

Do not forget to check the licence of the font you bought; verify that you are allowed to use it for the Web.

126

Typekit

Typekit is an Adobe product that allows users to ascribe a wide array of web fonts to their designs. The designer simply needs to create a kit by specifying which weights they would like to use and then supplying the URL of the site they will be deploying the fonts to. This process will create an embed code that can be copied into the header of the intended site, and then the fonts can be called through the CSS.

Other resources

If you own a font, you can convert it into .woff (Web Open Font Format); this is supported by all major browsers. There are online font converters such as Fontie web font generator, Webfont Generator, Transfonder, or FontLab TransType 4.

Slabo   Raleway

Source Serif Pro   Source Sans

Inconsolata   Merriweather

Abril Fatface   Lora

Lato   Ubuntu

PT Sans   PT Serif

Open Sans   Josefin Slab

Quicksand   **Roboto**

Acme   Arvo

Google Web fonts
A selection of fonts from fonts.google.com

Images for the Web

When using and creating images to be used for website design, there are a range of formats that differ from designing for print-based material. The image file size needs to be considered, as the larger the file size, the slower the website will be to load within the viewer's browser.

The first rule of using images within a website is not to scale the image to fit within the design layout but to work to the exact proportions of the overall design. For example, if the area on the website page for the image to fit into is 500 x 500 pixels, image-editing software, such as Adobe Photoshop, should be used to edit the image to the correct proportions; this will ensure that each image is being used at its optimum size for your layout.

Adobe Photoshop also incorporates a number of file options that can be used to save images for specific uses and displays within a website. The formats are all designed to compress and reduce the file size to once again enable the images to display and load quickly within the browser.

JPEG (Joint Photographic Experts Group)
Used predominantly for photographs and illustrations, this file is a 'lossy' format, meaning that the image you get out of decompression isn't quite identical to what you originally put in. Adobe Photoshop has options to check the quality of the image being saved in this format compared to the original, allowing you to control how much compression of the file is added.

PNG (Portable Network Graphic)
The PNG format is a 'lossless' format and retains all of the quality of the original file when compressed. The PNG format supports transparency and can be edited in Adobe Photoshop to cut out or erase an area of an image; if the image is edited on a layer and saved as a PNG, the transparency option is available to use. Once the image is placed into a website, it can be overlaid on a coloured background, and the colour would display around the erased area of the image.

Because it uses an alpha channel (transparency), a PNG contains a bit more information than a .jpg and is, therefore, a larger file. You need to consider this constraint when you have a lot of images on the same page as it can affect the page loading speed.

GIF (Graphic Interchange Format)
The GIF file format is used to display small animation sequences, for example, a rotating banner or a logo that text fades in. The animation usually only lasts for a few seconds and then repeats from the start as a looping sequence.

The animation is comprised of a series of still images that change over a number of frames and seconds, much in the same way as a traditional film sequence of images. The GIF format is mainly used in developing animated banners for advertisements for websites due to its compressing of file sizes.

SVG (Scalable Vector Graphic)
The SVG format is used when creating vector-based graphics such as shapes and lines created in Adobe Illustrator. When saved as an SVG the file consists of two parts: a code-based XML file (automatically written when the file is saved), and the image itself. SVG files are scaleable and retain image quality over a number of devices, from retina high-quality display mobile phones and tablets, through to laptop and desktop computers. For best results when creating graphics to use with the SVG format, try to keep the design as simple as possible, as the format does not support filters such as blurs or colour adjustments.

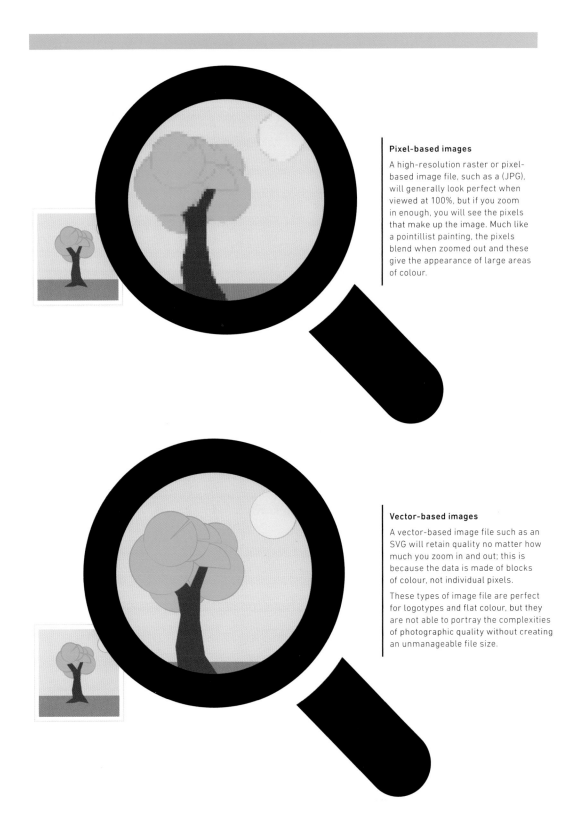

Pixel-based images

A high-resolution raster or pixel-based image file, such as a (JPG), will generally look perfect when viewed at 100%, but if you zoom in enough, you will see the pixels that make up the image. Much like a pointillist painting, the pixels blend when zoomed out and these give the appearance of large areas of colour.

Vector-based images

A vector-based image file such as an SVG will retain quality no matter how much you zoom in and out; this is because the data is made of blocks of colour, not individual pixels.

These types of image file are perfect for logotypes and flat colour, but they are not able to portray the complexities of photographic quality without creating an unmanageable file size.

Hand coding

Long before we had WYSIWYG HTML editors, web content was crafted by hand. In an effort to make the technology more accessible, digital interfaces were created that looked and acted much like page layout software. These interfaces rendered HTML files as the user dragged and dropped images, created text boxes and chose colour/font options from drop-down menus. While these interfaces succeeded in making the technology widely available, many programs had individual quirks that meant designers had to work in particular ways and did not have complete oversight of the process of construction. Additionally, many of these applications had unique ways of rendering HTML in the background and often added lots of unnecessary markup language.

There are now many more WYSIWYG editors, and these have grown to represent the challenge of contemporary web design. However, to have complete control over your project, learning to hand code is still, for many, the most satisfying way to progress a project.

Hand coding helps you understand the construct and meaning of the HTML you are using, and through that, intelligently identify a process that best fits your workflow and objectives. Having this control over your code and knowledge is especially important when it comes to solving problems, as an interface will not intelligently highlight problems or areas where the markup language can be streamlined. Also, handing off your front-end designs to a back-end developer will be a lot easier as you can work together to create a format and system that you both understand, and one that will also allow them to add their code without having to undo or alter your work.

Once you've learnt how to code by hand, you will likely drop the interface altogether, as the core tools you will need are a browser to check the files as you go, and a text editor to render the HTML and CSS.

Lastly, there are employability skills linked with the ability to code by hand. Software goes in and out of fashion, but hand-coding is essentially future proof — once you have learned this skill you can easily and quickly update your knowledge without also having to learn new software packages.

WYSIWYG editors

WYSIWYG (what you see is what you get) editors are interfaces that let you alter designs and add content directly through a login system that utilises the browser window. Elements may be selected and then transformed, adjusted, deleted or simply updated. These systems are especially useful for clients that do not have a great deal of technical ability and only want to make minor updates every now and then.

Typically, these types of systems would be custom-built by a developer to meet the needs of a specific client, but there are applications, such as Concrete5, that have in-built editors that work with a content management system. Both Drupal and WordPress fit roughly under this banner, as a range of alterations can be achieved without having to log into a back-end and adjust code.

Software

There are many tools available to help designers without knowledge of coding. Some of these applications are mainly visual and work to replicate the experience of working in InDesign or Photoshop, while others let the designer view and adjust the code. While these are useful tools (especially for beginners), they do have particular quirks in the way they render code, and very few offer the range of opportunity a designer possesses when they can fully control the code themselves.

Dreamweaver (developed by Adobe) is perhaps one of the most well-known editors; it is widely used because of its graphic interface and is, therefore, more familiar to InDesign and Photoshop users.

Brackets is an open-source text editor that allows the designer to edit code and then test directly in a browser. Many designers are also turning to Coda as it has a lot of inbuilt snippets that can be dragged and dropped onto an empty HTML document and, like Dreamweaver, it offers value suggestions, and closes tags.

As useful as each of these tools are, try not to get sold too much on one product. It is very easy to open HTML files and edit in any free text editor.

In-browser tools

A great way of getting to know HTML and CSS is to look at what other people are doing, and how they use the markup language. Every browser has a tool that allows you to get behind the scenes of a web page and the two most common (and useful) are Inspect Element and View Source. These tools offer designers the ability to see how others have arranged their code, what fonts they have used, how they have prioritised their CSS, etc. While this is a great way to learn, it is not good practice to take or 'borrow' another designer's code. While HTML and CSS might be open source as tools, the way a designer utilises them is not.

Debuggers allow developers to pinpoint faults that are not always easy to spot as you are working. This tool will shows you if you have not linked to a file correctly, if a file is missing, and a number of other simple errors that are easy to miss when you are dealing with a lot of code and markup.

SEO

SEO stands for 'search engine optimisation' – essentially this is the art of ensuring your website will be found and ranked highly by search engines. There are many ways of achieving this, and, unfortunately, these methods become redundant often as search engines tweak their algorithms and adjust the criteria by which they rank pages. There are a number of tools that a designer can employ to help with getting good SEO results, though it is a profession in itself!

Here are some basic things a designer/developer can do to help with SEO:

- Use the correct markup and follow the semantic conventions.

- Design for users, not search engines.

- Update the content regularly.

- Always use text for text-based content – never substitute text for images.

- Employ a clear hierarchy within your page design and link array.

- Don't obscure essential content by embedding it in rich media – this can't be indexed.

- Make sure you populate the `<header> </header>` on every page with a specific title.

- Give every image an alt tag and a descriptive file name.

- Give every page a simple and descriptive name.

- Use a consistent and easy-to-follow naming convention for your files – keep everything lower case and use em- and en-dashes instead of spaces.

- Test the textual content of each page to make sure if it is descriptive, legible and readable.

- Lots of people type in questions to search engines, therefore, an FAQ section is a natural link, as it may answer the questions being searched for.

- Develop sitemaps for each of the major search engines.

- Test your SEO, update your content and then test again.

- Always clear your cache and cookies before you search for your new page – cookies will record previous searches and give you biased results.

[See also: Critical discussions: Web 3.0: Semantic Web, page 156]

132

How SEO works

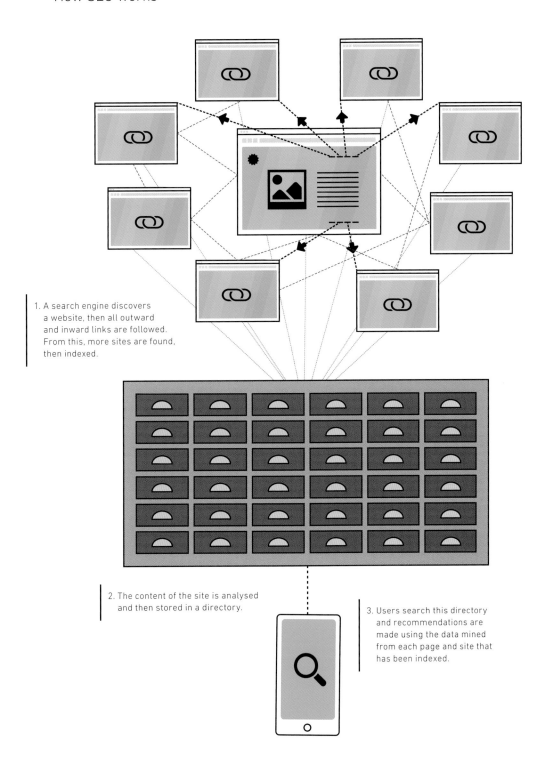

1. A search engine discovers a website, then all outward and inward links are followed. From this, more sites are found, then indexed.

2. The content of the site is analysed and then stored in a directory.

3. Users search this directory and recommendations are made using the data mined from each page and site that has been indexed.

How search engines work

Search engines work by sweeping the Web, crawling from site to site by following outbound links and steadily building an index. This process takes some time, so the crawlers won't always find a site immediately – it may take a few months. However, the more inbound links to your site, the more chance you have of being found quickly.

In addition to this, the main job of a search engine is ranking websites. When you search for a page, the results are presented in order, and this is achieved by considering the relevance and popularity – the search engine will firstly try to match the terms you have input for the search, and then it will rank the results in order of the popularity of the site, in the hope that the more popular ones are the most reliable.

The way this is all achieved is through an algorithm that is individual to each engine, and unfortunately, which is constantly changing. Though this is constantly changing, you can jump-start the search engine process by submitting your page to search engines individually (again, each has a slightly different process for this).

Keywords and page titles

Keywords are one constant that search engines use to rank your content and site. In the dark days of the Internet, people would add keywords as meta tags and search engines would use these to rank a site. However, many savvy web designers would add any popular keyword to their site in the hope it would propel them to the top of the list. All search engines have now disregarded keywords in meta tags and now look to content only.

When writing content, you should think carefully about the keyword searches people will undertake. Talk to your primary and secondary users to see what they would search for and the type of language they use.

People tend to be quite descriptive when searching, or they ask questions. While FAQs are a good way of answering question-based queries, good descriptive writing will help users find you via the content.

When writing about a service, go into specifics: talk about where the thing is, when it might be accessed – anything that is unique will help you more accurately meet the search engine query of an Internet user.

Similarly, you should always name your pages using clear and relevent terms, as this text is displayed in the browser toolbar, alongside a user's bookmarks. Perhaps most importantly, it helps search engines understand and classify the page. As an example, a simple and robust naming convention would be:

```
<title> About us - example.com </title>
```

Reading and using statistics

When you buy hosting, you will be given access to certain data via the control panel. This data (or analytics) can tell you what pages people are looking at and for how long (it's always less time than you would think!). It also tells you where in the world they are browsing from, the type of browser they are using and more.

Beyond this, the most useful information is normally how they arrived at your page. The analytics will tell you the search engine the audience used and what search they put in. You can also determine where they have come from if it is not search engine traffic – are there sites linking to yours, or has the user typed your URL directly into the browser address bar?

Once you know this information you can better judge the keywords you are using in your content – are they the right ones, and if so, can you do more of the same? Additionally, you might look to build relationships with sites that are actively promoting and sharing your content.

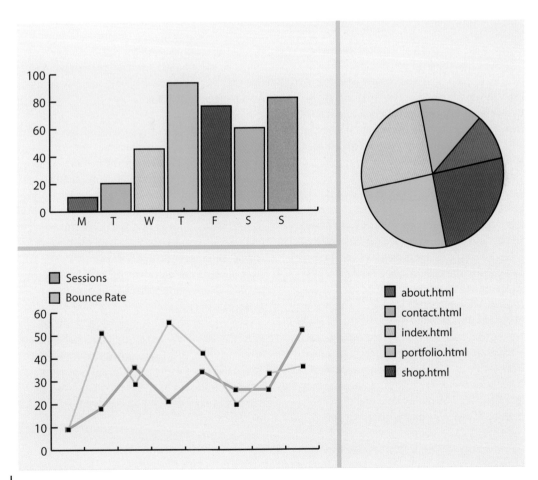

Control Panel

An example of a the type of data you may find in a control panel.

Critical discussions: Encryption and privacy

As a designer/developer, you have a commitment to your end-user that goes beyond the visual styling and the functionality of a web page or application, and that is to protect the personal data that you are entrusted with.

Every minute of the day, all around the world, people are sharing sensitive information across the Web and various applications. In a single online transaction, a person might share their financial information, date of birth, address and more. When applying for a job online, the applicant may be asked information about their sexuality, health, religion and other highly sensitive details.

Firstly, when designing a platform, you need to ensure that the data you are given is sent directly to you in the most secure way. This will likely mean that the user is offered the chance to create a password-protected account, and therefore, you can offer some guarantees that only the user and relevant people will be granted access to the content delivered.

Along the way you need to ensure that the data is protected by some method of encryption so if it is intercepted, it cannot easily be read. Data should also be protected by encryption when it is stored on your servers as hacks can happen, and you want to ensure that any information stolen during an attack cannot be read or used. However, it is important to point out that a lot of data theft is down to the carelessness of the people who have been entrusted with the data – for example, a person might copy sensitive information to a flash drive and then leave it on the bus, or someone could print an email that includes personal information, and then not dispose of this in an appropriate manner.

As previously alluded to, the storage of data is another consideration. While there is legislation in most countries that governs what can be stored, and for how long, ethically you should encourage your clients to consider scrubbing any stored information about their clients that is not absolutely vital to the business or is outside the scope of the original reason it was collated. The spring cleaning of data lessens the chance of it being used for purposes other than that originally intended, as it is simply not there to be accessed. However, even data needs to be disposed of in a thorough and appropriate way – if you put a computer in the bin, any person could scavenge it and access the data stored on the hard drive.

A company that collects email addresses should only store and use these if the person supplying the address has consented – just because someone has emailed you a query does not mean that they want to receive your monthly updates or news of special offers.

While many online services use carefully worded terms and conditions that cover the use of customers' and subscribers' data, increasingly many users are more and more concerned about how their private information is being used, and, therefore, want greater transparency. While people may not object to advertisers offering targeted advertisements based on their search engine, they might be upset if their views are shared with political parties they do not support or companies whose moral sensibilities they object to.

In July 2018, for example, some browser manufacturers decided to consider websites that do not use https as non-secure; subsequently, many sites started to encrypt their information to ensure they would not be regarded as hazardous.

Encryption and privacy
Every piece of data online will be protected by multiple levels of encryption and passwords.

Critical discussions: Marxism and the information economy

Marxism – developed by Karl Marx and Friederich Engels at the end of the nineteenth century, during the rise of manufacturing-based economy – is a conceptual framework (a system of concepts) that allows us to analyse society and history through the lens of the evolution of capitalism's mechanisms. Marxism addresses notions of class relations, social conflict, exploitation, alienation and ideology, among others. According to Marx, class struggle is inevitable, as the ruling class, which owns the means of production (from factories to servers), imposes its ideology on the working class and alienates them order to exploit them – the ruling class depossesses the working class population from both its work and the value of its work.

Economies and eras 1: Industrial revolutions, industrial ages

We talk about 'revolutions' because they happen in a short space of time, contrary to the slow pace of other developments. Such events have a rapid and durable impact on economical, societal, political, and technological developments. The Industrial Revolution occurred roughly between 1780 and 1820; it first happened in countries rich in coke (charcoal), and places able to export their produce, such as the Low Countries and the UK. The use of steam, the use of iron for all types of construction (rail, bridges, buildings) and the advent of machine tools, created new organisational methods of work and management.

This revolutionary shift resulted in a new type of worker, one Marx and Engels would label the Proletariat. In the UK, the need to sell off the goods led to the emergence of marketing during the end of the eighteenth century. The Second Industrial Revolution (roughly between 1870 and 1914) saw the application of gas, then electricity, to the household routine, as well as the advent of communication systems (e.g. telegraph, telephone, radio). The use

of petroleum in transport and factories marked an increasing rise in the speed of exchange, trade, and information. Both the First and Second Industrial Revolutions coincided with a significant development in territorial and economic expansion, imperialism, and colonisation. In the meantime, with full employment, local workers' conditions improved. In certain countries, workers, following the Marxism precepts, were unionised and sought to oppose the private corporations. In some other countries, corporations put on a more paternalistic role to provide their employees the commodities that would make their lives more comfortable, but ultra-standardised – they became the buyers of the goods they contributed to the production of (e.g. Fordism).

Postcolonialism

The oil crises of 1973 and 1979 occurred when the members of the Organisation of Arab Petroleum Exporting Countries (OPEC) significantly raised the price of the barrel. Most Western countries' economies were sustained by cheap oil imports; the sudden rise of oil price, concurrent to a shortage of easy ways to get charcoal, dropped those countries into a severe and durable recession. It was the end of the financial and economic boom, and also the end of mass consumption after the Second World War. The rise of the tertiary sector (the sector that provides services instead of producing goods) fostered the increasing importance of specialised education, and marks, to a certain extent, the beginning of the deindustrialisation in Western countries, where knowledge, information, and communication skills are now more valorised than physical labour.

Economies and eras 2: Information age and its new digital economy

The new economy, also called the 'digital economy' is a model that emerged during the 1980s, alongside the decline of Western countries' factories; it is a shift from an economy based on the production of goods, to an economy based on services; it relies on immaterial labour. The way people work in the digital economy is significantly different to how people worked during the industrial era. Mass production has been replaced by a more segmented market production, and the demand for employment flexibility has caused a resurgence in precarious jobs: part-time and temporary roles. The digital economy has also marked the rise of entrepreneurship culture (self-employment, freelancing) that glorifies merit, sometimes to the detriment of social equality. Nation states encourage private corporations by giving up regulations in order to gain favour within the global markets.

Digital labour

Antonio Casilli defines digital labour as value-adding activities performed by humans on the Internet platform (Casilli, 2017). Digital labour spreads from commenting on articles, liking a post, sharing a recent purchase, rating a service, answering a survey, retweeting an ad, creating a meme, playing with Artificial Intelligence such as Autodraw, to uploading a video or writing a Wikipedia entry. Digital labour encompasses activities we do online spontaneously, which we are not paid for but add value to the online product or service we are using.

For Christian Fuchs, whose perspective is anchored in the critical tradition (Marxism), digital labour is exploitation: companies make money at the expense of the users. For Henry Jenkins, champion of the participatory culture, the audience is keen and proud to share and to give for free what they like doing. On one hand, digital labour is a brand new aspect of capitalism, while on the other hand, digital labour

is considered a contemporary version of the 'gift economy', as theorised by the anthropologist Marcel Mauss (Mauss, 1925).

Microlabour

Digital labour should not be confused with Microlabour, a term coined in 2008. Microlabour designates a series of very small distributed tasks that, once put together, result in a unified project. Microlabour does not require a qualification, but it has to be performed by a human, mostly online. From a neoliberal perspective, microlabour is an easy way to earn extra cash; from a Marxist's perspective, microlabour is a new way to exploit low-income people, as microlabour often pays less than $1/hour.

Crowdsourcing

Crowdsourcing is an economic model that allows individuals and organisations to gather and obtain resources such as money, goods, commodities, services and even ideas, from the crowd – a large group of people, mostly Internet users. Crowdsourcing is used for idea competitions, innovation contests, genealogy research, astronomy (e.g. SETI project), among others. Some people praise the community spirit of crowdsourcing, some people argue that it lowers the quality of the final outcome, arguing the result will be homogenised.

One might question whether digital labour is a choice, as all online contributions may be considered as labour. Should your leisure time generate income for certain companies by tracking your browsing patterns and searches? Do you feel exploited when you recommend a purchase, share your address book to access an app or participate in a fanart contest?

Meet the designers: Do you code?

Inayaili de León, yaili.com

Yes, HTML and CSS, very little JavaScript. I even wrote a book about CSS back in the day.

Bruce Lawson

Yes, but not often any more; there are plenty of people better than me at coding, and I bring other skills.

Dan Hinton

Yes, I would comfortably call myself a front-end developer. I'm fluent in HTML and CSS, while also being comfortable working with Javascript and PHP.
I would say the fact that I do code is incredibly important, as it helps to provide a clearer understanding of how and why things work as they do.

Ricky Gane

My coding levels are only very basic HTML to piece an emailer together.
I think it's important to have an understanding of the coding process if you are working in digital. Be kind to the web developers and they will give you all sorts of useful tips on how to design things so as not to give them a headache later on.

Sush Kelly

Yes – although I am definitely more front-end than a back. I am comfortable in HTML/CSS and JavaScript and can stumble round a little PHP. As a freelancer you can't just pass a task over to someone else so you end up learning a little bit of many things. This is good though as it gives you an appreciation of what is possible.

Sylvie Daumal

No.

Understanding how code works is definitely mandatory. You must know the principles and the differences between the different languages. You must be able to talk with the developers and CTO. However, being able to code is less important than being able to think, create, test. It's a nice-to-have skill, not a must-have.

Ross Chapman

Only when I need to! I taught myself HTML and CSS when I used to customise WordPress sites for clients. Nowadays, I just use it for updating my own website. The prototypes we create within Sprints don't need code, as they're just a smoke and mirrors version to validate what we want to further design and produce, so it's not a necessary skills in my particular role.

Nodesign

Yes. To work in the digital industry, you should know at least enough to be able to understand how digital technology works.

Amy Parker

Yes: HTML and CSS so I can prototype interfaces in a browser. Thinking back to when I didn't code, my process was so excruciating because it was so repetitive and I spent so much time creating documentation and managing files instead of just creating. Even though my code doesn't always make it to production, it's so exciting to control what's on screen and see a thought or a sketch come to life.

Jamie Homer

To code or not to code? That is definitely the question! I can code – to an extent. It's definitely worth diving in to for a better relationship with your developers, but I do prefer to let people do what they are best at. I say let the developers develop, let the designers design.

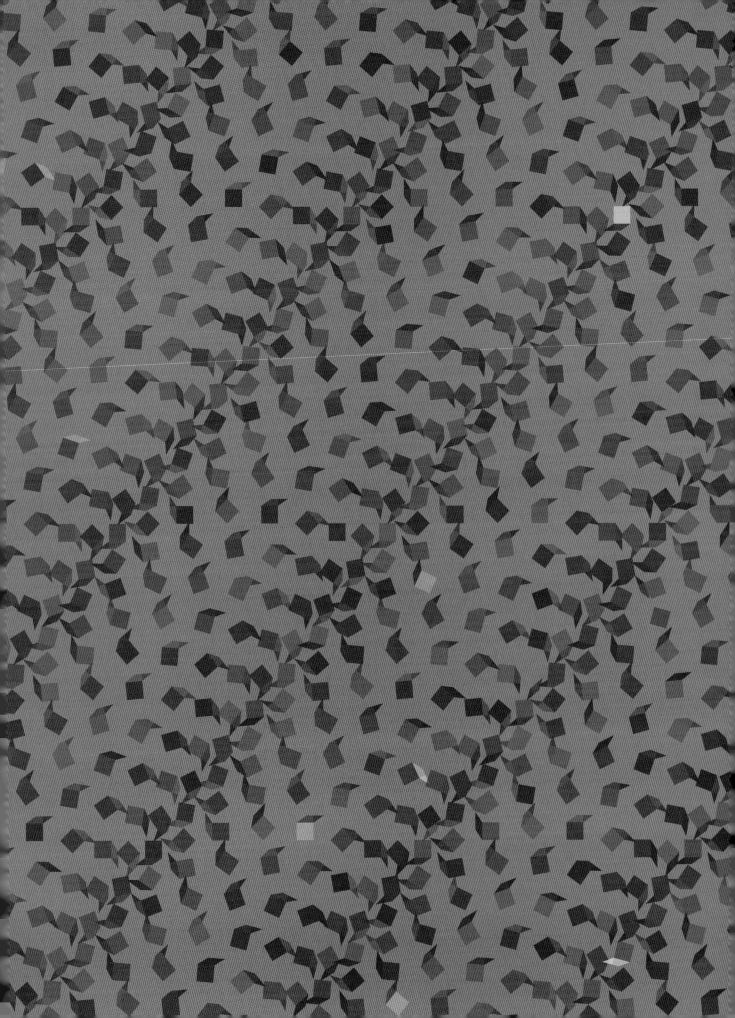

CHAPTER 5:
WEB 2.0

For too long, the Web was a presentation of information akin to the most basic presentation of printed material. While hypertext links meant that information could be accessed in a non-linear fashion, that didn't herald the birth of new ways to present the content within. Starting with forums, chat rooms and later blogs, Web 2.0 brought great change, and offered the user the ability to adapt, play with, create and comment on content – this is the true democratisation of online data, and one of the most exciting web-based developments since the birth of HTML.

Layouts for the Web

The first websites were technical considerations, and design was a secondary thought. As websites became more consumer-facing, design became more important. The first 'designed' websites were essentially a graphic designer transferring their knowledge of design for print to the online environment. Pages were designed like pages from a book or magazine, and the web page was treated as a fixed piece of work to be printed, but with hyperlinks.

Fixed layouts were okay to a point because most people had similar-sized browsers, and certain rules for the fixed layout were devised (largely, these have all now been superseded). 720px x 460px was a recurring design canvas because this is the space that the designer was left with on screen after you took out the loading bar, the scroll bar and favourites.

However, gone are the days of traditional fixed website design. The death of fixed layouts came about because designers could no longer predict the canvas size users would view their work on. All websites will be viewed on a number of devices, so a design has to cater for all of these ratios and also future-proof itself for the next generation of devices and monitors.

One might argue that accessibility and the content of the site are more important than design features.

Responsive layouts

Design elements will respond differently depending on screen size – elements might look lost because of the amount of space the screen offers, they might be crammed in because of a small screen ratio, or worst of all, elements might be cropped or left unreadable on a small mobile device.

Responsive design saves creating different designs for devices, or specific mobile sites.

You may reshape, resize, or show and hide elements depending on the screen capabilities of a particular device. Essentially, when the browser does not have space to show two elements side-by-side, you will create a CSS rule that states one should move beneath the other. This work is done using media queries.

A media query will enact a unique set of CSS rules that are linked to the current screen ratio of the device your site is being viewed on. You may create rules for desktops, laptops, tablets and mobiles, and would normally also create more conditions for portrait and landscape viewing.

The example shown opposite is a media query that offers two size options for the 'section' element of a web page. Here the desktop and tablet version comes first ('section' is 700px wide), then the query (for the mobile version – you will notice the screen width is specified) offers an alternative sizing.

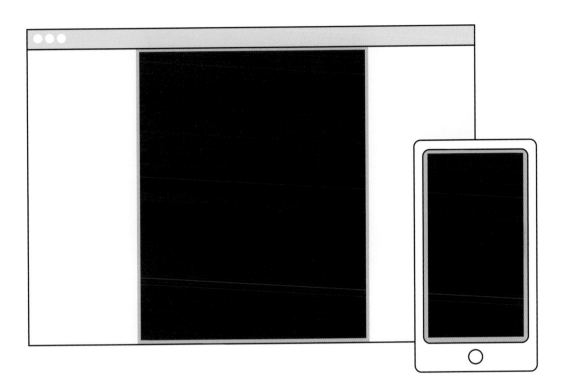

Example responsive layout

The layout above is a basic one column responsive layout. The 'section' area has been assigned a width of 100 pixels, and without a media query, the section would always display at this size, irrespective of browser and device size.

The section is centred in the page as the margins are set to auto - no matter how big the browser window is, using this will always ensure the content is in the middle of the page.

The media query here is important as it will look for certiain events (here a browser window that is less than 350 pixels wide), and then employ changes such as changing the width of elements, moving and hiding elements, or actioning other CSS rules.

```
The CSS:
section {
              width: 700px;
              padding: 10px;
              margin: auto;
}
@media screen and (max-width:
320px) {
              section {
                      width:
300px;
                      padding:
10px;
                      float:
none;
              }
}
```

Adaptive layouts

Adaptive layouts are similar in some ways to responsive ones, but the emphasis is more on reshaping content than completely restyling it.

Working with percentages is often the most straightforward way to approach adaptive design. This method will allow you to take up a specific proportion of the browser window rather than a fixed pixel value. It allows for more variation than responsive design, and in that way, it is future proof.

However, adaptive designs will need some limits, as 100 per cent of a browser open on a super desktop will look very different to 100 per cent of a browser on a tablet device. You don't want your design to get too wide and distorted – this will create unreadable line lengths and mean that you have to use really large images to take up the space available, or else you will be left with gaps.

```
body {
  width: 100%;
}

nav {
  width: 46%;
  float: left;
  padding: 2%;
}

header {
  width: 46%;
  float: right;
  padding: 2%;
}
```

Even with this method, you will normally use some parameters and might employ:

```
Max-width: 960px
```

With the previous CSS rule, the content will grow up until a certain point. With the following example, the content will get no smaller than this value but can be bigger.

```
Min-width: 300px
```

Further media queries

Below is an example of a media query you might couple with the last snippet. This site will grow to 100 per cent of the space possible using the last bit of CSS, but this media query will make sure the content does not fit edge-to-edge on a mobile device and allows for some margins.

```
@media screen and (max-width: 320px) {
  body {
    width: 96%;
    float: none;
    padding: 2%;
  }
  nav, header {
    width: 100%;
    float: none;
  }
}
```

Essential code 'viewport'

Mobile devices will attempt to shoehorn a website to fit its screen size; if you want your design to adapt (as a responsive or adaptive design) to the particular screen's ratio, you need to tell the device to treat every pixel as a pixel, and not try to fit several into the space of one.

```
<meta name="viewport"
content="width=device-width, initial-
scale=1.0">
```

[For more examples, see: www.wdgd.co.uk]

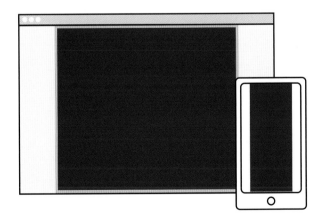

```
section {
  width: 100%;
  padding: 0px;
  margin: auto;
}

@media screen and (max-width:
320px) {
  section {
    width: 100%;
    padding: 0px;
    float: none;
  }
}
```

```
section {
  width: 70%;
  padding: 1%;
  margin: auto;
}

@media screen and (max-width:
320px) {
  section {
    width: 70%;
    padding: 1%;
    float: none;
  }
}
```

Grids

The grid system originated within the design of publication and print and was developed to create a cohesive design format that produced a logical structure of typography and images together. The 960 grid system was developed for website designers in an effort to streamline web development workflow by providing commonly used dimensions based on a width of 960 pixels.

The 960 grid is a width that is suited for the wide number of platforms on which we browse the Web. It essentially allows for a 1024px wide monitor to show the site accurately and without horizontal scrolling, accounting for the width of the browser chrome, scrollbars and a bit

of padding for legibility. There is always a ten-pixel margin placed at the right and left of the main content column, which means that smaller browsers will always be able to read the farthest left content without the text butting against the browser window.

The grid is divided into a range of pixel widths, across twelve, sixteen or twenty-four, equally sized columns; for example, in the twelve-column grid, the narrowest column is sixty pixels wide. Each column after that increases by eighty pixels. Similarly, in the sixteen-column version, the narrowest column is forty pixels wide and each column after that increases by sixty pixels.

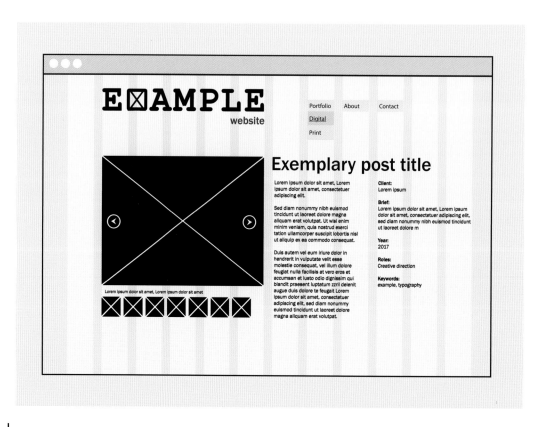

Grid systems
Much like a printed page, the most organised web pages rely on an underlying grid system.

Bootstrap

Originally created by a designer and a developer at Twitter, Bootstrap has become one of the most popular front-end frameworks and open-source projects in the world.

Bootstrap was created at Twitter in mid-2010. Prior to being an open-sourced framework, Bootstrap was known as Twitter Blueprint. A few months into development, Twitter held its first Hack Week, and the project exploded, as developers of all skill levels jumped in without any external guidance.

Bootstrap utilises a series of CSS (Cascading Style Sheet) classes, that are defined in it, which can simply be used directly to build a number of online web solutions over a range of hardware devices, from desktop to mobile. Since version 3, Bootstrap utilises a framework that consists of 'mobile first' styles throughout the entire library, instead of in separate files, allowing the designer to develop websites or mobile applications from the smallest screen first.

Bootstrap is supported by all of the popular browsers and contains a range of functional built-in components that are easy to edit and customise, as well as a range of predefined themes and templates.

At its core, Bootstrap can be defined by three main files: bootstrap.css – a CSS framework; bootstrap.js – a JavaScript/jQuery framework; and glyphicons – an icon font set.

Additionally, Bootstrap requires jQuery to function. jQuery is an extremely popular and widely used JavaScript library, which both simplifies and adds cross-browser compatibility to JavaScript.

By using Bootstrap's own predefined CSS classes, even for the aspiring novice writing and developing websites or applications, this is a good introductory route with a wealth of online documents and tutorial videos to get started.

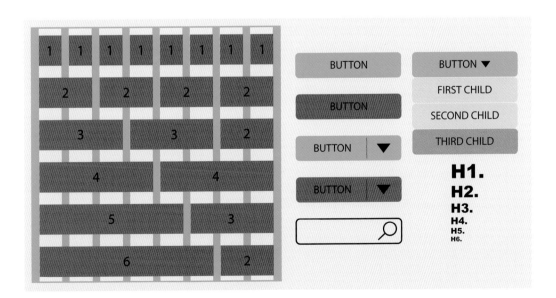

Bootstrap framework example

The image above shows an example of a simple Bootstrap framework. This combines information that is pertinent to the use of a grid, and CSS rules that are developed from a Style Tile.

Content management systems

CMS (or content management system) describes a type of website that allows the client to make regular updates and add content in a way that is not too dissimilar to updating a blog. As long as there have been websites, clients have wanted to update their own news sections and add products without having to call a developer in.

A CMS allows the client to login, and depending on the system, they will be given certain rights and privileges.

Designing for a CMS site can be a challenge as normally the designer/developer will start with a design that has content in place, or else they will be issued assets to use as content. With a CMS build, the designer/developer will often start without content.

CMS solutions

CMS systems rely on templates to ensure that users with little or no coding ability can use them to get a site up and running. When we hear the word 'templates', alarms sound (think Excel!). However, there are many CMS systems that employ very usable, functional and well-designed templates, which are perfect for everything from small portfolio sites to online shops and blogs. One of the best aspects of many of these themes is they built in ability to adapt to screen ratios – this saves the designer/developer a massive amount of work and means they can concentrate on integrating the customer's brand, typographic styling and layout options.

There is an ever-growing list of CMS solutions available to developers and designers. Some of the most popular include:

Cargocollective.com
Cargo offers a range of themes that are highly creative and versatile. They are all easy to manage and can be adapted if you have some HTML and CSS knowledge. You can apply your own URL to your Cargo page, and become part of their community.

Squarespace.com
With Squarespace you have access to a range of well-designed themes and also the facility to add a blog and webshop to your online presence. You can customise every part of your website and have full access to analytics for your page.

Format.com
Aimed specifically at creatives, with Format you can choose from a range of themes and use their WYSIWYG editor to adapt every part of the page. Additionally, you can add an online shop, edit HTML and more.

Indexhibit.org
Created by Daniel Eatock and Jeffery Vaska, Indexhibit allows you to create simple, fuss-free pages for free. Simplicity really is at the heart of this system, and it is very easy to use, set up and manage. However, it doesn't offer the functionality of some of the other systems.

WordPress.com and WordPress.org
WordPress is perhaps the most powerful and well-used CMS platform, and it has two very

different options. With WordPress.com you can register a blog, apply your own URL and choose from thousands of themes. WordPress.org allows users to download the source files and host them on their own space. By hosting WordPress yourself, suddenly the scope of what can be achieved broadens. With a self-hosted system you can access many more themes, write your own theme, add an online shop and access a massive stockpile of plug-ins that will add extra functionality to your pages [for more, see: Themes and plug-ins, page 154].

Drupal.org

Drupal is an open-source system that works well for large-scale sites that have a number of users. Used by government and educational bodies, it offers a range of themes, integration tools and add-ons.

Magento.com

In terms of e-commerce CMS builds, Magento is a very popular system used by a range of high-profile retailers. Again, this system is open source and offers a wide range of themes and add-ons.

Joomla.org

After WordPress, Joomla is perhaps the most used CMS system on the Web. Similar to Drupal, it is great for large sites with multiple users. It is open source, and there are many free plug-ins that can be added to the system, which allow for greater functionality.

Concrete5.org

Concrete5 was developed to be easy to use. Unlike many of the other CMS systems, you edit directly on the page rather than having to go through a back end.

TinyCMS.eu

TinyCMS does exactly what the name suggests – it is a CMS system for small websites. It is also much smaller than other similar systems in terms of disc space taken up. Like other systems, it uses short codes as a way of the user bringing in more functionality to their layouts without having to understand HTML.

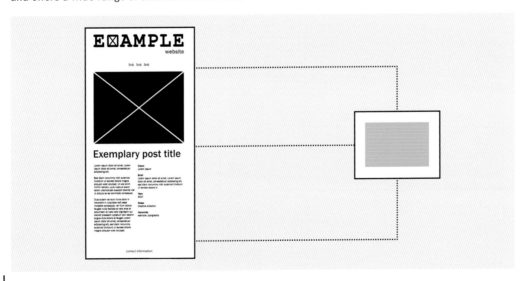

CMS theme linking to a database

No matter which CMS solution you choose, all will have a unique way of linking to a database to populate your pages with content, and an interface that allows a user to author new content.

Themes and plug-ins

As mentioned previously, themes are one way of cutting down on your workload, and by extension, this creates more affordable solutions for clients.

Most modern themes will be developed with responsive and adaptive concerns addressed, and a great deal will include extra functionality such as e-commerce, galleries, etc.

All themes will be customisable to an extent and allow the user to change or add logo, colours and typefaces. However, if you want to add extra functionality to a page you might look at plug-ins for an equally affordable solution.

Plug-ins will vary depending on the CMS package you are using, but normally they will integrate with the theme and system of choice and allow for extra functions in the front and/or back end. With a system such as a self-hosted WordPress site, you can add plug-ins that can bring through a social media stream to your site's footer, a gallery function to your portfolio pages, or even create custom post types in the back end to allow for more possibilities and classifications when posting content.

How a CMS theme works

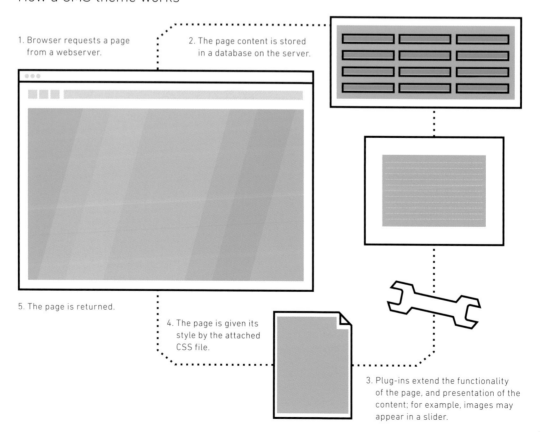

1. Browser requests a page from a webserver.

2. The page content is stored in a database on the server.

5. The page is returned.

4. The page is given its style by the attached CSS file.

3. Plug-ins extend the functionality of the page, and presentation of the content; for example, images may appear in a slider.

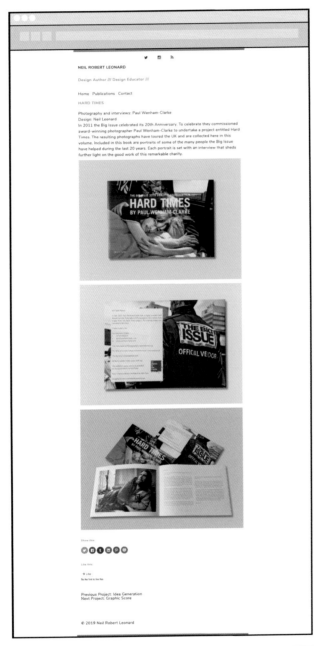

Neil Leonard

neilrobertleonard.co.uk

Design and construction by Neil Leonard with Alex Bradbeer

The simple WordPress template is made up of only a few parts, but with plug-ins and widgets, it is infinitely extendable.

Top right: The homepage calls a preview of the most recent posts. Each post preview consists of a featured image and its title. While this design is kept purposefully minimal, the preview could also feature other data such as a post excerpt, authors name, date of publication, tags, categories, and more.

Top left: This is an example of a post. Once the user has clicked on a post preview, it will link to the content. The post content is retrieved from the database and the information displays in a post template – unlike a traditional HTML website, you only need to design one-page layout and set CSS rules that dictate how the content is displayed.

Bottom left: WordPress has built-in customisation tools, but this theme includes additional unique options such as the ability to add social media icons and links to the top of each page using the customiser rather than a plug-in (too many additions such as plug-ins can slow loading times and frustrate users).

Critical discussions: Web 3.0: Semantic Web

The Semantic Web aims to turn a web of documents into a web of structured data related to each other.

The increasing amount of information circulating on the Web leads pioneers such as Tim Berners-Lee and others to propose an extension to the Web standards. The implementation of this new standard (the Semantic Web) is meant to improve information reliability and relevance, assist users in their search for information and reduce their dependency to search engines' opaque algorithms.

The Semantic Web relies on an extended set of specific metadata attached to each media by content producers. It also relies partially on folksonomy, which is a portmanteau word between 'folk' and 'taxonomy'; it refers to the way end-users manage knowledge, the way they associate one piece of information to another, how they organise and classify information and how they retrieve it. It is also called collective intelligence. Folksonomy is both the Semantic Web's strength and one of its weaknesses: it supposes that every user thinks and organises knowledge in the same way, and it also assumes that everyone will 'play the game' by adding metadata relevant to the topic.

The Semantic Web is designed to be readable by both machines and humans; it is a compromise between natural language (the way we talk, the way we ask questions) and code (the way machines compute data). Firstly, that makes the input process easier – content managers and content curators do not have to 'speak machine'. Secondly, it facilitates the output, since the machine can answer questions asked by the end-user (semantic query) in a way close to natural language. Finally, this feature of the Semantic Web helps machines to communicate with each other, boosting data indexation efficiency.

The Semantic Web's aim is to have a world of data that is open – not privatised nor monetised.

The Pompidou Centre website in France and the BBC website in the UK are good examples of Semantic Web for knowledge management. By allowing their visitors to add metadata to their resources, from paintings to documentaries, they facilitate new idea association, new paths between artists, mediums, techniques, epochs, places and themes. These websites enhance navigation possibilities and are not limited to one website but extend, thanks to linked data, too many web domains using the same standard. These websites foster free knowledge acquisition, and the more websites that use the Semantic Web, the more the networked data realm will be accessible to the public with ease.

Data.gov.uk and Data.gouv are good examples of the Semantic Web used for knowledge representation. By opening public data to developers, governments allow the latter to give new meaning to sets of data that otherwise would have been simply stored in stacks for administrative purposes. The Semantic Web relies on developers (and designers) to turn rows and columns of data into some artefacts and graphs that make sense for the public.

In detail, the Semantic Web is composed of Resource Description Framework (RDF), which is a standard model for describing resources; Web Ontology Language (OWL), which is the Semantic Web language designed to represent rich and complex knowledge about items, and their relations to each other; and Extensible Markup Language (XML) that could be connected to a database.

While a non-semantic web page's tag would look like:

```
<item>post</item>
```

A semantic page would be encoded in this way:

```
<item rdf:about="http://example.org/se-
mantic-what/">Semantic Web</item>
```

Yet, the Semantic Web has opponents. Because its implementation requires the restructuring of whole websites, it is considered as heavy investment. Additionally, because it facilitates the aggregation of fragmented sets of information left on the Web by contributors, it could be considered a governmental tool, used to monitor a country's population.

[For more, see: https://www.w3.org/standards/semanticweb/]

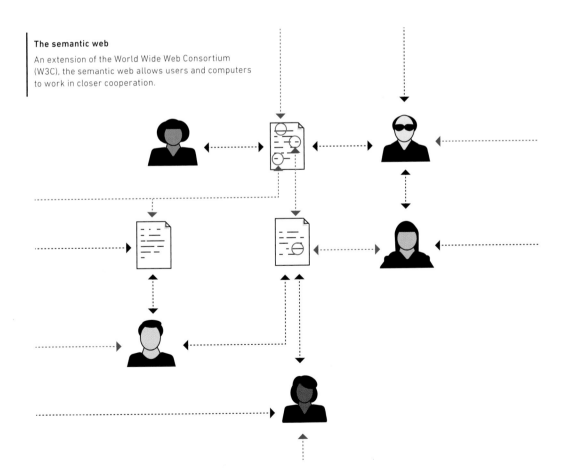

The semantic web
An extension of the World Wide Web Consortium (W3C), the semantic web allows users and computers to work in closer cooperation.

Critical discussions: Open Internet and Net neutrality

Net neutrality is part of the open Internet notion and is a founding principle of the Internet; there should not be any discrimination to the access of data on the network – Internet service providers should not restrain the content of downloaded or uploaded data; should not:

- restrict the content of downloaded or uploaded data

- discriminate against any communication protocol (www, email, FTP, etc.)

- discriminate sender or receiver

- degrade the content of exchanged data.

Yet, since 2000, selective management systems of the network are technically possible: data flow could be filtered and packets of information discriminated in favour of their senders, receivers or contents. What has been developed mainly to stop virus spreading and prevent hacking may have become economical and political tools. What may be at stake is free movement of ideas, freedom of speech, knowledge circulation, free entrepreneurship and, on a long-term basis, the ability to innovate and social development.

According to its founders, the Internet was designed to be an open network and should be considered as a public utility, like water, electricity and gas suppliers. Giving access to everyone is part of the democratic momentum of the Internet, and founders claim that this is endangered by both discriminating business models and censorship. Proponents of the Net neutrality regulations argue that, from an economical perspective, discrimination of content may imply that only a few who can pay Internet service provider fees for privileged access, could use the whole potential of the network and its resources (music and video streaming, peer to peer file sharing, social media). Furthermore, the big companies such as the GAFAM (Google, Apple, Facebook, Amazon and Microsoft) already operate as a monopoly, would pay Internet service providers to be accessed faster than smaller businesses. They also argue that, from a political perspective, sender/receiver discrimination may mean that users can access only government approved information (banishment of certain social medias, applications and/or websites). Incidentally, some governments already use Internet policies to monitor populations and shape their opinions.

Opponents of Net neutrality regulations, which includes corporations, economists, Internet service providers and technologists, argue that raising fees for a heavier usage of the bandwidth will prevent its overuse and will guarantee its availability, especially in troubled periods such as a natural catastrophe or terrorist attack. They also argue that, on the model of tiered services for mobile phones, it is fair to charge users in relation to their bandwidth usage and then to use profits to invest proportionally in new technical features, and to sustain innovation when and where it is needed. In the spirit of *laissez-faire* economic liberalism, opponents of Net neutrality regulations are against the intervention of government bodies in the free and open digital realm.

Proponents recognise that there may be some limits to the neutrality depending on the context; in periods of congestion due to natural catastrophe, it may be important to give advantage to rescue communication channels in order to guarantee the availability of the bandwidth, but reasonable network management practice rules may do this job.

The debate about Net neutrality is not closed; while alliances are agreed between corporations and some Internet and mobile providers in underdeveloped countries to provide users with access to one small piece of the web (e.g. Facebook zero, Google Free zone) for free, governments are still considering whether or not they should interfere with the market economy. After having established the Open Internet Order in 2010, the US government, via its Federal Communication Commision (FCC) decided to repeal Net neutrality, in November 2017.

Should the Internet be considered as a public utility? Should you pay more when you watch a movie online than when you read your emails? Should some corporations be given greater access if they can pay for it? Would you design a service that promotes a 'closed Internet'?

Pay-per click

Net Neutrality allows users across the globe equal access, regardless of status and wealth. Many are concerned about the privatisation of the Web, and the possibility that users will be charged for access (paying by the minute, or byte, for example).

Meet the designers: What are the tools of your trade?

Inayaili de León

I always like to have a pen and paper at hand, preferably Sharpies and Post-it notes. Digitally, I like iA Writer and Simplenote as they can sync between devices. I also use Google Docs and Office 365 quite heavily. When it comes to visual work, I mostly use Figma — I like the collaboration features and how I don't have to deal with files on my computer. And when it comes to code, I've been using Visual Studio Code. I track my to-dos in Things and Microsoft To-Do. And I have the Dictionary app open at all times.

Bruce Lawson

Twitter, Github, and knowing lots of people, so I know who to talk to about what. I'm also never afraid to ask questions.

Dan Hinton

It will come as no surprise that Apple devices are integral to my day-to-day activities, making use of a MacBook Pro for the heavy lifting and an iPhone for the managing of clients. Software wise I still use a fair amount of the Adobe Creative Suite, but I'm gradually moving over to more and more independent apps. Of most interest is Coda (used for coding) and Sketch (used for digital design).

Ricky Gane

I have a dual-screen set-up running on a Mac Pro, a good speaker system for previewing audio, headphones so I don't annoy everyone else at work (also handy for blocking them out!), a Wacom Intuos for precision control and a LaCie Rugged lightning drive for working locally on large projects. On the software front I mainly use the Adobe Creative Suite (mostly After Effects and Premiere Pro), Cinema 4D for 3D work and Vectorworks for architectural interiors.

Sush Kelly

I have a real thing for notepads and pens, so they are always to hand. From there, Sketch, Illustrator and Photoshop are my most used graphic tools. Being able to prototype ideas quickly and get them into a browser makes iteration of a design or idea really quick.

Sylvie Daumal

The software tools used by the team are Sketch/Invision/Zeplin, as well as the Adobe Suite and the Microsoft Suite, but the most important tools are pen, paper and sticky notes.

Ross Chapman

Now these are likely to be quite different to other designers. I use frameworks like the Design Sprint and tools like user testing to get design done right. I have a few other tools handy, pretty much all based in the cloud, but a Time Timer and the right team is all I need to get the real work done.

Nodesign

A Mac, electronics, programing, WeIO (our own electronic platform for IOT prototyping), 3D-printer, home-made laser cutter and PCB printer.

Amy Parker

I (almost) always start everything I do with a sketch (or at least a handwritten list) so my sketchbook is my number one tool. I use Illustrator for working out bits and pieces of look and feel, colour palettes, typography, and graphic elements of an interface. Atom is my code editor because it's the first code editor I ever used and I haven't had any reason to switch. It auto-fills in code for you which is especially helpful when you're learning to code.

Jamie Homer

I think it would be very difficult for a person to be involved in the creative industry without citing Adobe's Creative Cloud offering as being pretty much at the top of their list! My go-to software for writing code, uploading and interacting with FTP file spaces are anything by Panic Software (Coda or Transmit) and BBEdit. The other tools that I couldn't forget are a sharp mind that can become immersed and obsessed with any area of interest, a propelling pencil, and of course my trusty square grid Moleskines!

CHAPTER 6:
RICH CONTENT

The rise of social media has brought with it a need for content that is fresh, exciting and immediate. It needs to engage and entertain an audience on the go, and be shareable. This advent and change, alongside greater access to the Internet and faster connection speeds, has meant that more video content and messaging has been developed and now features consistently on most web platforms. In addition to the growth of motion-based media, interactive videos engage users through storytelling and play – these are two very useful devices for clients needing to capture and keep viewers.

Social media

The term social media refers to a range of platforms that allows users (or customers) to stay in touch with friends and family, whilst also providing enough personal information to allow for targeted advertising. The platforms are low cost, easy to use and have massive reach. Therefore, it is easy for start-ups to reach a large audience with little effort, and for established companies to reach even greater numbers of potential customers. While all platforms offer the ability to add textual content, visual content such as photographs, animated GIFs and videos are more likely to grab the attention of users and engage them. The ability to like or follow a profile and see recent updates can easily be integrated in a website using many of these platform's inbuilt tools.

Facebook was perhaps the first major social media platform to explode worldwide (unless you count MySpace...), attracting users from all parts of the globe, from all types of backgrounds and all age groups. It is easy for users to start a page and share news with friends and family. It is equally straightforward for businesses to start a business page and attract 'likes'. A like will help track fans and potential customers, and your updates will appear in a person's social media stream alongside news from their close social circles.

Twitter is a microblogging platform that constantly updates as people tweet. In terms of functionality, there is little difference between a tweet from a friend or a tweet from a company, as the ability to share images, video and text apply to all, as does the limit of 140 characters. However, businesses can deploy sponsored tweets that can be targeted to reach users in specific locations, or with certain interests, and by many other means. Users following an account on Twitter would expect it to be updated regularly, normally once a day. The immediacy of Twitter is its main unique quality, and a stream integrated into a website makes it look busy and provides fresh content.

Instagram is predominantly a visual social platform. The focus is on images and short videos and, like Twitter, these are very much in the moment. Filters can be applied to content to make images look vintage, retro, aged, or simply to improve the original picture through cropping, rotating and adjusting contrast. Much like the other platforms, companies, friends and relatives will appear together in a user's stream. This platform is particularly effective as it relies on images, and the user does not need to read, they only need to react to the visual content.

Any social interactions offer possibilities for longer-term relationships with customers – a 'like' or a follow will place you in a person's social stream, and their consciousness, permanently.

Video for the Web

When broadcasting a message, video is very effective, and it tends to engage viewers far more than static and textual content.

One of the major advancements in terms of creating video content came not from the content itself, but from the opportunities afforded by broadband – it suddenly became much quicker to load videos, and potential customers were not lost due to long waits as a preview of the content (let alone the content itself) began to download.

As mobile networks increased their capacity, it became possible to watch streaming video on a device, such as a phone or tablet, without buffering or waiting for content to load. This development led to the increase in usage of video on social networks, and for many companies, this is now the primary mode for advertising messaging in this context (perhaps even above text and images).

Social networks and blogging sites such as Tumblr, also led to the rise of Animated GIFs. Twitter and Facebook users often use animated GIFs to express their emotions or thoughts, normally with a healthy dose of irony.

The downside to creating video content is that it can be a costly venture, and this expense can be prohibitive when a company is new or does not have a large marketing budget.

Panic Studio
Bit Of Healthiness (Images, this page and previous)
Client: Ignilife
Panic Studio teamed up with Ignilife to create an introduction video for their white label app in France. Panic felt the video was the most effective way to interact with Ignilife customers, as if offered many opportunities to display information in an engaging way.
www.panicstudio.tv/en/works/vigisante-app

Interactive content

By definition, nearly all content on the Web is interactive. All pages will likely involve some interaction in terms of basic scrolling and clicking, and many contemporary sites offer more advanced user interaction that is made possible because of constant advances in technologies.

Initially developed by Macromedia, Flash is an application that allows a designer to create animated and interactive content for the Web by utilising a timeline that will be familiar to users of After Effects, and ActionScript coding language. ActionScript can either create linear interactions (a button leading to a specific place), or more open-ended gameplay. With Flash, you can easily code quizzes, puzzle games, first-person and platform games, and more.

With Flash, a designer can incorporate video and sound into their designs with ease, and for many designers, this used to be the go-to tool for creating interactive content. However, usage of Flash has decreased in recent years due to the lack of support on widely used devices and the advances in HTML5 and CSS3.

Much of the interactive possibilities that were once only achievable through the use of Flash can now be achieved by using a combination of JavaScript, HTML5 and CSS3. Java has always offered interactive functionality, but the introduction of JQuery [for more, see: JQuery, page 98] has made this more accessible to designers. There have been some issues with regards to devices and the compatibility of Java, but largely it is a safe and comprehensive tool to use.

CSS3 alone offered a great amount of activity. With a click, users can alter objects by transforming them, adjusting size, scale, opacity and colour. All of these effects can also be triggered by utilising the timeline features.

Sound for the Web

Sound can be a very important part of developing content for the Web when it comes to instructing a user, or signalling interactions. A sound effect makes the push of a button sound 'real', and a particular 'ping' has become synonymous with the arrival of a new email. In our daily lives, our own hardware platforms, desktop, tablet and mobile all have technology that uses sound in unique ways. Sound on web pages is a very controversial subject. Many people hate sound of any kind on a web page, and even people who don't mind sound tend to hate automatic background music – especially if there are no controls to turn it off. So, before you add sound to your site, you should be very sure that it serves a purpose and adds value to the content.

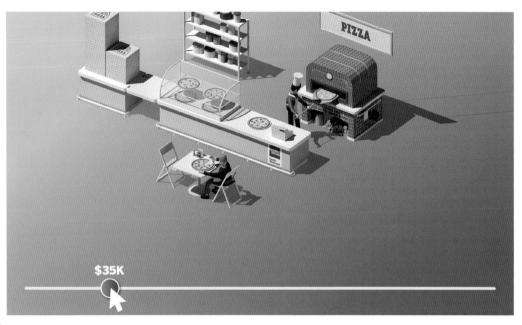

Panic Studio

AMEX - Let's Get Business Done

Client: Bajibot

Designed in collaboration with Ogilvy and Bajibot's creative teams, Panic created an interactive animation-based social media campaign that clearly explained the loans to the customers of Amex Merchant Financing. The content shows customers what different levels of loans might offer their business in a visual way that cannot be successfully demonstrated with the written word alone.

www.panicstudio.tv/en/works/amex

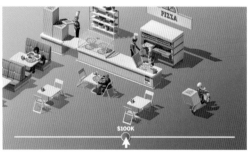

1.

Voice Over:
Let's be honest, everyone loves travelling...

Visuals:
We see one end of the table full of travelling equipment, and a figurine of a panda with bobbing head...

The camera starts to pan to the right.

2.

Voice Over:
...but planning and booking?

Visuals:
...and at the other end of the table there is a mess of travel guide books, printed pages with hotel offers, and many other little notes.
The camera starts to pan down in the line with the table leg.

3.

Voice Over:
It's too easy to get lost in the vast and uncharted lands of the internet...

Visuals:
The tables leg morphs into the waterfall. We see a traveller get out from behind the bushes in the left corner of the screen, and then the river going far away into the horizon. The river branches out on both sides, and at the top of those branches we see the holograms of different travelling offers (from flight, car rental on the hotel booking ending).

4.

Voice Over:
...while looking for the best deals.

Visuals:
We find the traveller lost and nervous in the dark forest, surrounded by a huge amount of "fireflies" which keep on buzzing and blinking, trying to aggressively catch his attention. One "firefly" (in 7ojozat colours) start to slowly and calmly fly to the traveller.

5.

Voice Over:
But fret not!

Visuals:
The "firefly" lands on the man's hand and we see him looking at it curiously, while the "firefly" keeps on glowing warmly.

6.

Voice Over:
7ojozat is here to guide you.

Visuals:
The hologram with the logo of 7ojozat starts to project from the "firefly".

7.

Voice Over:
Need to quickly find a hotel...

Visuals:
We see the traveller going through a dreamlike land full of hotels which are floating in the air. The "firefly" flies away and starts to turn into a star.

8.

Voice Over:
...with the best reputation?

Visuals:
The stars start to fall from the sky, and lining up at the top of the buildings looking like rating on booking websites.

9.

Voice Over:
Plan and book a journey for your WHOLE family?

Visuals:
The traveller pulls out the phone, and on the screen we see a picture of the happy family on a trip in Paris.

10.

Voice Over:
...

Visuals:
The camera starts to zoom into the smartphone.

11.

Voice Over:
And like to have a huge pool of deals to compare from, without feeling overwhelmed?

Visuals:
Inside the smartphone we see a neatly organized offers for hotels, car rentals and flights.

All of the windows start to gather in the middle...

12.

Voice Over:
At 7ojozat.com you have everything on one page.

Visuals:
...and morph into one. The logo of 7ojozat animates in.

Motion-based content

Motion-based content has been used within website design in various formats since 1994, and the initial content was used as website advertising banners. These small adverts were created as animated Gifs using bright colours and simple animations to attract the viewer's attention. Due to the slow connection and transfer speeds of data at this time, file size had to be kept to a minimum, and this restriction meant that motion content was kept to simple fade-ins of text, or movement of an image horizontally across the screen.

In 1996, a company called Macromedia developed software called Flash. Flash was designed specifically to develop animation that could combine interactivity, while keeping the file size to a minimum. At the time, Macromedia Flash became one of the most popular platforms in developing motion-based content. In 2005, Macromedia's rival, Adobe, purchased the software and continued adding and developing new features. In 2016, Adobe changed the name of the software to Adobe Animate, and included a range of new features such as the ability to export animation as HTML and high-resolution 4k video.

As technology has developed and access speed of the Internet has become faster, the development of motion-based content has increased to allow designers to utilise video and animation in a much more dramatic and compelling way, with browsers displaying full-screen video and animation that is interactive and engaging to the viewer in a number of ways. Instead of the traditional use of navigation, such as buttons or links, viewers are now introduced to interactive stories that are nonlinear, and allow the viewer choices in progressing through the content in alternative routes.

With designers now able to add various types of coding to layers within the video or motion-based content, some clothing and fashion outlets online now offer the shopper interactive videos of the clothes. This technology, called 'motion tracking', combines motion content with invisible buttons that move with the video. This can, for example, be displayed through models and fashion catwalks, where the viewer can view video footage of the clothes being worn which is selectable, and once clicked, options for purchasing the clothing are displayed.

In education, motion content and interactivity are also combined together to create learning experiences for children; traditional cartoon-style characters and stories now contain selectable options, that from an early age, can help develop key skills in spelling through both interactive motion content combined with sound.

A trend that has become popular since 2010 in website design is the use of parallax scrolling to navigate to each section of a page. Parallax scrolling is a technique where background images move by the camera slower than foreground images, creating an illusion of depth. The website is designed as one long page, each containing a section of information; when a navigation button or link is selected, motion is applied, which moves the page to the relevant section.

BluBlu Studios

Client: 7ojozat

BluBlu created this design-driven animation for their client, 7ojozat, the first hotel booking search engine in the Middle East – it is the Arabic leader in online bookings. This work delivers the clients message in a compelling and effective way, immediately capturing the viewer's attention through its use of colour, characterisation and motion.

www.blublustudios.com/portfolio/7ojozat

Web docs and the Cloud

The 'Cloud', or 'cloud-based computing', gives users the ability to store or edit documents online, that can also be shared and distributed by others. Social media, such as Facebook, uses the same type of technology when viewing friends, posts and timelines, reflecting the concept of a shared network. Google and its own cloud-based storage system, called Google Drive, allows the user to store data such as images and documents, which can be distributed with the authorisation of the owner. This can lead to collaboration by groups of people to edit and read documents anywhere in the world.

As cloud technology becomes more prominent, cloud-based software has been developed by companies to allow people to share information in a business or working environment, under the heading of collaboration tools. When teams use the right tools to work together, they often make improvements in both the process and the final outcome. Using the right online collaboration tools can make teams stronger and more productive. GitHub is one such tool

that allows coders and developers to share and download source data, which can then be used within their own code-based applications. While others have a more specific role, such as project management software, this can be used by a team to set deadlines and monitor goals of individuals working on a project.

Basecamp is one such collaboration tool that allows users real-time tracking of project deadlines and outcomes, share files and schedule meetings. This enables teams to work much more productively and efficiently.

As with any data that is shared and hosted online, the use of the Cloud poses ethical questions regarding who owns the data and who is in control? By putting data or services in the Cloud, the user gives up much of the control they might have expected if they had kept the data within their own organisation and network. This discussion is an ongoing one for the pros and cons of cloud computing.

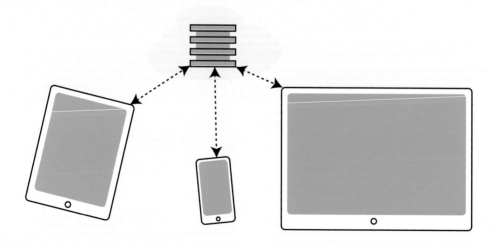

The Cloud

Documents stored in the Cloud can be accessed and edited on multiple devices.

Banners and (targeted) advertising

Anyone who has used social media, such as Facebook or Twitter, will instantly recognise banners and targeted advertising. These small adverts are usually placed to the left and right of the main website content, and for an average blog or website owner, they can generate a reasonable income.

For example, an advertiser or company has a product or service that they want to promote to the optimum amount of people – and they want these to be the right people, so they would pay for space on a relevent website or blog. Users visiting the website or blog will then see advertisements targeted at them; this is judged by the relevance of the advertisement to the site, or the interest defined by the user through their search engine history, cookies from sites they have recently visited, or content with companies via social media sites they may be logged into.

This is referred to as the 'Pay Per Click' model – the publishers are paid a small amount for every user who clicks through from their platform to reach the content designated by the advertiser or company.

While some see this form of interest and cookie tracking as invasive, younger Internet users tend not to be so concerned – in fact, many like to see advertisements that are targeted specifically at them.

However, one major issue with this model is the likelihood of average Internet users reaching new content and discovering new brands that are beyond the scope of their previous search and browser histories.

Banner advertisements

Banners and targeted advertising will be a familiar sight. As web users hand over more data through Internet searches and browsing patterns, these advertisements become increasingly specific and individual.

Critical discussions: Art on / with the Internet

Summarising Internet art in one single section is a challenging task. Art on the computer did not start with the Internet; the first computer poem was 'Stochastische Texte' by Theo Lutz, in 1959. In 1960, Brion Gysin developed his permutation poem 'I am that I am' with Ian Sommerville. Artists such as Nam June Paik and Roy Ascott, explored telecommunications and developed their own practice too, while electronic and technological tools were used to spread live performance.

Since the 90s, Internet art has been fuelled by various artistic frameworks: Dada, situationism, conceptual art, optical art, kinetic art, video art, game art and performance art.

This should not be confused with art displayed on the Internet; physical artwork digitised and uploaded on a web gallery is not considered Internet art. Internet art needs the network to exist: the network (beyond the World Wide Web) and its technical and logical potentialities are one of the main components of the artwork; notions such as immateriality, interactivity, global reach, connectivity and performativity are the core of the Internet artwork.

Internet art includes, among others, ASCII art, Flash art, digital poetry, net art, generative art, glitch art, art mode, game art, etc.

It is an art that is sometimes called 'media-specific'. In this sense, it questions and challenges the historical monopoly of art galleries and museums within the art system: art experience is now not only accessible but delivered through the Internet. Internet art escapes to its traditional intermediaries.

Internet art is engaged with Internet technology, its societal impact and its aesthetics. Through art, we can question the increasing dominant role of search engines in accessing the net; by making Internet art ubiquitous, we can question the notion of distance, public space and privacy; by bringing people together, Internet art allows us to investigate the notion of community, but also the notion of digital identity online, and it allows us to challenge perceptions in virtual environments. Internet art could explore the boundaries of surveillance and control, and experiments with proliferation and visualisation of data; because its code is sometimes replicable, sharable, modifiable and its content remixable, Internet art also challenges the notion of authorship, uniqueness and authenticity.

Finally, since Internet art relies (but does not depend) on a constantly evolving environment, it also questions the preservation and archiving of new media art.

What do you think of an art practice that questions new technology, and what in contemporary society might be the focus of the work?

Garrett Lynch IRL

Wasting Time on the Internet

Image over (top): Wasting Time on the Internet.tiff

Wasting Time on the Internet is a performative process demonstrated through a photographic weblog based on Kenneth Goldsmith's theory and publication.

Image over (bottom): A network of people who attended an exhibition and contributed to the creation of this work.

A network of people who attended an exhibition and contributed to the creation of this work shows the social networking of attending an art exhibition employed to create an artwork.

www.asquare.org/

Wasting Time on the Internet

About   participate   help

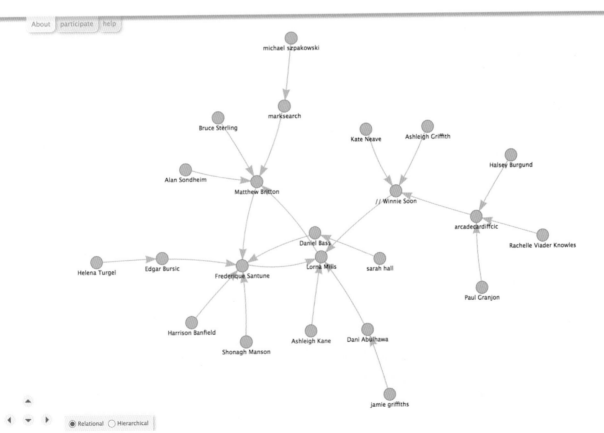

Relational   Hierarchical

Meet the designers: Which soft skills are important in your role?

Inayaili de León, yaili.com

Writing is a core skill, especially in a role like mine that involves a lot of documentation, guidelines, and sharing of knowledge. An understanding of good design principles, what makes a good design, and being able to spot patterns and connections is core to anyone working on a design systems team, but also a degree of selflessness and humility. A lot of the work we release and champion is not necessarily 'ours' – it's good work that is done in different teams that can be elevated and shared by the system.

Bruce Lawson

The ability to research – either for a talk, doing competitive analysis, analysing a specification, or writing an API. A large network, and listening to people.

Dan Hinton

Problem-solving and people skills. All the important work comes from both of these, as whatever the project or brief is, you're fundamentally there to solve someone's problem. You also need to be good at reading people, taking what they want and crystalising into something that will work. One personal skill I rate very highly is self-awareness. Knowing when to stop talking and stopping yourself talking bull, can be the difference between winning and losing a client.

Ricky Gane

You have to enjoy what you do; if you don't enjoy it, there's no point. Getting stuck in is a given too – no one likes a lazy b*****d! It also helps to have a good sense of humour.

Sush Kelly

The willingness to learn is the biggest thing for me. The software lifecycle means that as designers and developers we have to stay up to speed on programs, languages and even the approaches and standards of modern web design. I learn something every day without fail and even though I am senior in most teams I work in, quite often a junior will have an idea or workaround that I will take on board. There is always something to learn.

Sylvie Daumal

The ability to listen and learn all the time (and enjoy it), to generate and try new ideas without fear. The drive to create excellence for your client and never stop.

Ross Chapman

I think technical ability is overrated. I'm way more interested in finding people that are comfortable in their own skin, bring something new to the team and have a drive to learn new things. Tools can be picked up and skills can be learned, but bring your personality and be yourself. More and more, being able to talk to people and sharing knowledge is becoming important and moreover speed of getting things done.

Nodesign

Culture, curiosity, empathy, artistic skills and sensibility.

Amy Parker

Communication! Being able to explain the role of design and convey design concepts to non-designers is crucial.

Jamie Homer

More and more agencies are hiring people that fit with their culture, over and above the quality of their work. They view the quality of work as something that can be nurtured, whereas the personality, ethics and approach of a person are often far more set in stone. So if people are looking for a digital agency to join, make sure to do your research first to see if the fit is not just good for the agency, but also for you!

CHAPTER 7:
THE ROLES

As digital possibilities develop and broaden, so do the associated roles. Here, we will explore the numerous avenues a person may take as they embark upon their career in the digital industries. We will look at the roles in broad terms so that you get the fullest picture of what is available to you, enabling you to make the right choices.

Designers

The way a designer works on interactive, Web and digital projects will vary greatly from studio to studio. Some work in a very integrated way, whereas others take the old-fashioned approach of supplying a developer with Photoshop files.

As Web and digital design has become more of a singular industry (in contrast to the way it was offered as a bolt-on to other traditional print and advertising services), designers have constantly looked to adapt the way they work, to ensure swiftness of the process, and so that the client gets the solution they need. More and more, this has meant embracing basic code and working closely with back-end developers to ensure that ideas can be developed, tested and designed, all at once.

Gone (largely) are the dark ages when a client would be asked to sign off a design by looking at a static PSD file; they will now have the chance to preview a digital solution at each stage of its development.

Rather than guessing how a flat image might look in the browser, modern agile methods mean the client will be able to preview and test rough wireframes on a number of devices from the outset.

At this early stage of testing, UX developers will be working out the best possible viewer journey, and the ideal way for them to access information; then UI developers will be looking after the look and feel. Beyond this, there are a myriad of other tasks happening, and these essential cogs do not have to wait for a PSD to start turning.

A digital design team at work

Designers preparing to take their paper-based concepts to the Mac.

Photography credit: Andrew Way and Alexander Lucas

Developers

Back-end developer

The back-end developer will have a range of high-level computer programing skills that could include: Java and C++ and PHP. Data that is added from the front end of the website by the user is responded to by the back-end developer's coding, and usually, an action will take place when the user inputs their data.

For example, a customer that interacts with a shopping website may initially set up their account and details, including name, address, and contact details. This is stored within the back end of the system, and as the user buys items from the website, this data is then assigned to their account.

Other complex data routines are also collected as the user interacts with the site, such as calculating purchase information, delivery time slots, payment, and verification details of the user's financial transaction. The back-end developer is also responsible for testing the data handling systems that have been developed and put in place for the user, to make sure the functionality and collection of the data works across all of the systems engaged with.

Front-end developer

The front-end developer role, or client-side developer as it used to be called, is the term given to the role of producing HTML, CSS and JavaScript, one that the viewer of the website can directly interact with.

As technologies change with the development of mobile platforms for viewing and interacting with the Internet, the role of the front-end developer constantly changes and adapts to this, problem-solving how to best utilise adaptive and responsive design, and dealing with the wide range of screen sizes on mobile phones and tablets. Developers have to be aware of various technologies and trends in the planning and development of websites. The initial goal of the developer is to ensure that the structure and design of the site is cohesive and logical in its arrangement of navigation, content and information.

When developing the site, the front-end developer always has a clear set of goals in the initial stages of the developmental process at the starting point, these are:

- Cross-platform – will the design layout and structure be cohesive across a range of computer systems?

- Cross-device – will the site be accessible on a range of devices and sizes of screens, from computer to tablet and mobile?

- Cross functionality – how will the site perform through a range of browsers such as Chrome, Safari, Firefox, etc.?

- Accessibility – how will the user interact with the site? Would they be using a mouse, keyboard, touchscreen? What is the size of the platform, computer desktop, mobile device (i.e. phone or tablet)?

All of these need to be considered within the functionality of the design and content, and all come with a unique set of problems for the developer to overcome when designing the structure for the content.

User experience designer (UX)

The role of the user experience designer is a relatively modern evolution, and it is one which has been brought to the fore by the increasing development of new digital services.

With the range of mobile platforms used to engage audiences with websites and applications ever-increasing, the user experience has become paramount in how the viewer engages with the content in the most seamless way possible.

The user experience designer's role can be compared to developing a roller coaster. The user interface designer builds the roller coaster, and the user experience designer is there to ensure the 'experience' of riding the roller coaster meets the expectations of the target audience. In the case of a roller coaster, the excitement, thrill and adrenaline rush, are all part of meeting the target audience expectations, and on a website, the interface, structure and content of information are no different.

The user experience designer will work closely with the UI designer and other members of the team – gathering information from the public, testing the usability of the website before it becomes live, assisting within the design development stages, and looking at the potential target audience and its relationship to expectations of how the content will be structured.

UX, as a part of the design process, is often misunderstood, as too much is expected from it. UX is not a series of magical recipes that allow the design team to save time, it is a process that questions every aspect of the end-user journey. Answers should be unique to each product/service and each client.

User interface designer (UI)

The user interface designer's role is much closer to the traditional role of the graphic designer. The UI designer works closely with the UX designer in how the overall content and interface will develop, considering the look and feel of the website or application.

Content, interface and the design itself need to be considered for a range of hardware platforms and browsers; what works well on a computer desktop will need to be reviewed when navigating a mobile phone, with the interface and content developed in a much more sympathetic design.

Some of the responsibilities of the UI designer can include: UI prototyping, interactivity and animation, adaptation to all devices and screen sizes, implementation with the back-end developer. As a visual and interactive designer, the UI role is crucial to any digital interface and to how the final user interacts with the information.

When the design is well-structured, the user interface becomes almost invisible or second nature to the user, with the information and content of the website or application being absorbed in a seamless way. If the user has to stop and 'learn' how to navigate the interface, then in some ways the UI designer has disrupted the experience of the end user.

BOND

WAASTAA – Creatives unite!

WAASTAA is a visual directory to the makers of the world. Users can discover hand-picked creatives in cities around the world and collaborate with them in real-time. WAASTAA is the user's very own visual diary, keeping them in the know for can't miss-events by creatives in their own city or anywhere in the world.

Bond Abu Dhabi and Helsinki teamed up to create the concept for the app together with the client. Bond designed the user interface, user experience and onboarding flow of WAASTAA.

Futurice was the software development partner.

The app utilises light and simple user interface, keeping the content of the users as the main focus point.

www.bond-agency.com/project/waastaa/

Motion designer

The motion designer's role moves away from the traditional role of the graphic designer, and takes the skills of typographical design, layout and image into a moving environment. Motion design has evolved as a direct result of technology improvements, and as desktop computers have become more powerful, the creation of motion graphics and video editing has moved away from high-end specialist equipment.

Motion designers utilise areas such as time-lapse, stop motion, animation and video, as well as specialist software such as Adobe After Effects, Premiere Pro and Animate, to construct a motion graphic product that communicates messages through movement. All of the skills and theories from graphic design can be used and applied within motion graphics.

Outputs of work from motion graphics can be used in websites as animated banners, TV adverts or films. Title sequences rely heavily on the principles of graphic design such as legibility of type to the viewer once movement is added, use of colour combinations etc.

Put simply, they design graphics that are in motion – just as their title suggests. Other skills the motion designer needs are a good grounding in animation and moving-image concepts, and narrative and storyboarding from paper to digital outcomes.

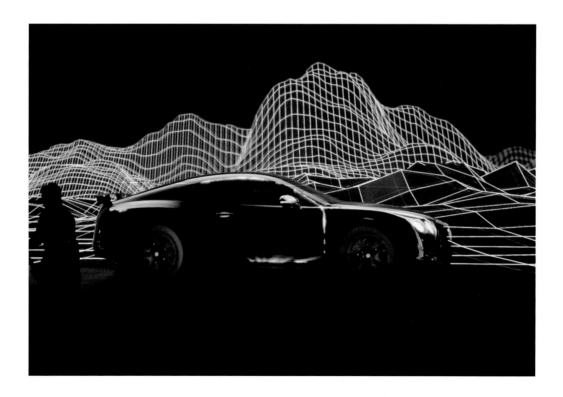

AGGRESSIVE

Bentley 'A Legacy of Performance'

From the Blower to the GT3-R, Bentley has always thrilled discerning drivers with their dramatic, race-ready dynamics. Aggressive's projection mapping performance at the Bentley Pebble Beach 'Concours d'Eleganc' Lifestyle Event introduced guests to this powerful legacy while setting the stage for the reveal of their newest model.

Created by a team of motion designers, and projected onto a white-wrapped GT3-R and a 30-foot backdrop, Aggressive crafted an iconic, art-inspired interpretation of the brand's essence, historic milestones and racing spirit, all framed against handcrafted 'engine-revving' audio-design and music.

www.aggressive.tv/projects/Bentley

Creative director

The creative director sets the overall vision and strategy for the project, guide the team, time manage, and set goals and deadlines to keep the team on track through each of the stages of development for the project. Creative directors also liaise with the client and inform the client of each stage of the project, updating and presenting the work that the team is producing.

The role is multiskilled: a good creative director will have good people management skills, as well as a discerning eye for good graphic design.

Building a network of multiskilled specialists around the role of the creative director is an important one, as each design project can vary, and the creative director, in some cases, needs to be called on for specialist support on individual projects when needed.

For example, a video to promote a car manufacturer will need a team of video directors and film-makers. The creative director would brief the team on what was required and discuss the final outcome for the film.

Information architect

The role of the information architect can be a complicated one to define in some ways, and sometimes the role of the information architect is shared within the design team that are developing the project.

The simplest way of defining the information architecture role is 'the organisation of the information and content received from the client'. This is then developed into a clear logical structure that informs the UX and UI designers as to the hierarchy of content. For example, the client could be a company that sells shoes online – the structure of the information is paramount in the development of the experience and interface design to the user of the website.

The information architect would need to structure a websites information into categories, for

example male/female groups of shoes, age range and colour or styles. The main categories would have subcategories, and the information would be displayed in order of importance and relevance to the user.

Some of the questions the information architect needs to consider are: How will the user flow through the information? How does the website capture the information selected by the user? How is this responded to and displayed back to the user? Is the information viewed informing the user in a decision-making process?

Collaboration with the user experience designer can be vitally important at this stage of development in order to produce a positive and meaningful structure of content for the user of the website.

Account manager

The account manager is the link between the client and the sales team within the design studio.

This person usually maintains a relationship with the client throughout the project, and if the relationship is an ongoing one, the account manager would consistently be assigned the same client each time, to generate a positive experience between the company and the customer.

The account manager serves to understand the customer's demands, plans how to meet these demands, and generates sales for the company as a result. Account managers need to understand and establish the budget for the company and the project; manage and solve any conflicts that may arise with the client; make sure deadlines are met for client accounts; and have good communication and people skills.

Copy and content manager

Copy and content managers oversee the information that is incorporated into a digital environment. The role can involve discussions and collaboration with the client in developing the content, and making sure the information is formatted correctly, approved and ready to be added.

These managers should have excellent organisational skills and the ability to meet deadlines; the ability to build relationships with clients and partners; a good grasp of English grammar, punctuation and spelling; and creative skills to find interesting ways to present information and to generate new ideas.

Copy and content managers can deliver information to a range of digital information channels such as websites, apps, social media posts, digital brochures, blog articles, and so on. The role could include collaboration with external specialists, such as photographers and film-makers, to obtain content.

183

Strategist

The role of the strategist is to analyse the goals, opportunities and challenges of all aspects of a business. Some of the skills required by the strategist include seeing how decisions and choices affect the long-term viability and the overall effectiveness of an organisation, and being able to analyse statistical and informational data to make informed solutions. They will also help cross-functional teams develop and evolve ideas to bring together brand goals, retailer objectives and consumer needs.

Areas of the role can include competitive analysis and identifying gaps and opportunities in the marketplace – essentially looking to innovate and keep the company at the forefront of emerging behaviours, technologies and ever-changing business models.

The strategist will select appropriate frameworks, tools and approaches to use in solving problems. Strategists will work in collaboration with teams, confidently presenting their findings to clients.

Community manager

The community manager's role is relatively new within the industry, and sometimes job skills can cross-over into the areas of the copy and content managers. The community manager can be the face of the company, working to create relationships, both virtual and physical, and ultimately build the company's brand, both online and off.

Some of the tasks within the role can include public relations, managing incoming media requests and building relationships with industry journalists and thought leaders.

Events are very important in terms of this particular role, and by extension event planning.

Hosting and attending industry events or meetups for the community are a good way to showcase the good work being done by the company, as well as seeking out new opportunities.

Skills needed for the job role can include having an outgoing, confident personality. Community managers will be required to walk into networking events and be comfortable introducing themselves to strangers. Public relations experience, great time management skills and the ability to multitask are all important traits for a community manager, since they're managing so many different areas of the business.

Marketing

The role of marketing can be defined in terms of customer needs and satisfaction, how a product can be presented to an audience through a number of promotional channels.

Marketing projects are usually delivered by teams, the members of which have various specialist skills in research, promotion and social and print-based media. Designers, developers, photographers and film-makers may also make up some of the specialist skillsets needed in the production of marketing material.

In terms of delivering a website to a client's potential customers, marketing can mean defining the target audience, and goals for the website, what information is being communicated, and what this means in the relationship to the customer needs and satisfaction.

Marketing can involve researching the client's competition within the market and offering solutions regarding what makes their client's product unique.

Market research may be conducted in various ways, through customer focus groups, testing, round-table discussions, or surveys. This gathering of information helps to understand the customer needs, and focuses the marketing on specific goals for the product.

Once this information is analysed, specific marketing solutions can be developed and created to communicate the information about the product to the customer; this can range from advertising through print and digital channels, such as social media, through to product launch events and product placement within shopping retailers both online and off.

AGGRESSIVE

Nikon 'Generation Image'

To illustrate how outstanding Nikon photography transcends
the ever-increasing stream of tens of thousands of images
created every second by today's generation, Aggressive
collaborated with McCann Erickson to craft a visually stunning,
projection mapping driven marketing campaign.

www.aggressive.tv/projects/nikon

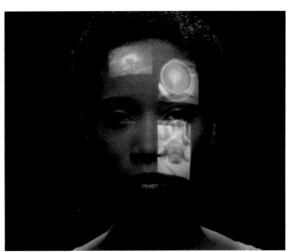

Critical discussions: Feminism and Intersectionality

According to the UK Commission for Employment and Skills (2015), the female national employment rate is 47 per cent, and while there is no job shortage in this sector, only 26 per cent of those working in the digital and creative industry are females, and about only 3 per cent of the creative directors are female.

By contrast, a British study undertaken in 2015 (Universities UK, 2015) demonstrates that in art and design, there are more female than male students.

Where does this striking discrepancy come from? What impact does it have on visual communication in general and in digital media in particular?

In the 1990s, gender studies researchers demonstrated that gender identity is a social construction: we are driven to match what we believe society expects from us, depending on our biological sex. Under the pressure of the social conventions (parental education, educational institutions and media that promote patriarchal ideals) we are raised in, we will be expected to be sensitive and to look for protection if we are biologically identified as a female. Conversely, we will be expected to be strong and take the lead if we are biologically identified as a male. By extension, women are encouraged to accept patriarchy as if it was the 'natural order', and are therefore encouraged to stay at home raising children while men are the breadwinners. In an environment where a career choice depends largely on a biased perception of gender, women tend to limit themselves; this is called the 'glass ceiling' effect.

Despite this, history gives plenty of examples of women who have succeeded in escaping society's imposed stereotypes, and who have had satisfaction in their public and intellectual lives, their work, their family life and their sexuality.

Educators need to carry on promoting these success stories until these successful women are no longer an exception. In graphic design, we might mention Paula Scher, Jessica Hische, April Greiman, Susan Karr, Margaret Calvert, Jessica Walsh, and Johanna Drucker among others; in digital technology, we will list names such as Ada Lovelace, Grace Hopper, Anita Borg, and Carol Shaw.

What would it change within the visual and digital communication landscape if there were more women involved in the design team?

Maybe some products would be more relevant to their usage and less stereotyped. You can still find some articles online explaining that a website whose main audience is women should be simpler because women do not understand complicated navigation.

If more women worked in the graphic design industry, we might stop hearing about 'feminine' (i.e. curvy) typefaces and pink being a colour for girls. The study of semiotics tells us that these connotations are learnt and arbitrary, and a more diverse workforce would help with the questioning of these stereotypes. A sign does not exist alone, and meaning cannot be constructed without people agreeing on a shared understanding of the object, typeface, or colour. The meaning-making process, depends on the arrangement of a set of signs, therefore, meaning can grow and change if a designer questions their toolkit and challenges the status quo.

The story of feminism started long ago; women have been fighting to be considered as equal citizens since the seventeenth century, if not long before. In the 1910s, they finally won the right to vote in the UK; during the second wave of feminism in the 1960s and 1970s, women fought for their liberation (access to contraception means, legal abortion and access to the job market). The 1980s backlash underlined the narrow scope of a fight that was mainly focused on heterosexual white women, and in the 1990s, the battlefield widened and became what is now is called intersectionality – the overlap of different social identities humans are made of, encompassing not only biological gender but also sexual orientation, social background, ethnicity,

nationality, religion, age and disabilities, or any combination of these.

Do men, women and people who are gender fluid currently recognise themselves in the depictions that the media make of them? What are the limits of gender-targeted marketing? What would be the impact of having more diversity in the visual communication industry? How do we invert the dynamic?

What does it mean to be a feminist in graphic design nowadays?

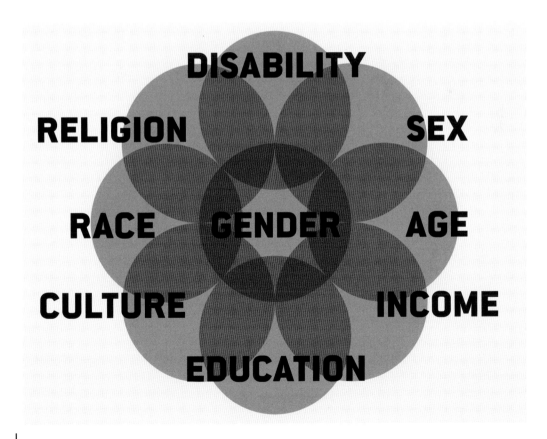

Intersectionality

This diagram shows the intersections between the many identities that make up any one person – we are all more than one thing, and out identities are a complex and rich mix.

Meet the designers: How did you get to where you are?

Inayaili de León, yaili.com

Writing has been a crucial part of my career trajectory. I've had my blog for many years, and have been writing about my work since the beginning. I've been a guest author in several online and printed publications, which gave me visibility, and signals that, as a designer, I can describe problems, talk about my process and work, and make a case for it. This skill has been vital for every job I've had, and for my career as a public speaker, and it's essential for any designer.

Bruce Lawson

Blogging. I had a blog about accessibility and web standards in 2004, which got me recruited to join Developer Relations at Opera. That got me officially in the world of standards and browsers. I wanted to learn (and contribute) to HTML5, so started to rewrite my WordPress blog in HTML5, blogging about it and giving feedback to the spec authors. This got me a book deal, which led to lots of invitations to speak at conferences. Honestly, sharing your knowledge and perspectives is a great way to help others, and boost your own profile.

Dan Hinton

I took a less conventional route into the industry by starting up a company straight out of university – it really isn't as hard as some may think and I always wanted to be my own boss. I'm very much of the mindset that starting something after graduating is one of the best times to do it. You have no financial and family commitments, which makes the prospect of earning very little money at the start possible.

Ricky Gane

I met a friend who gave me the details of his Studio manager – I contacted him straight away. I hadn't even touched a Mac at that point, but explained that I had a positive attitude and a real desire to learn. He agreed to give me a week's unpaid work experience. I must have made a good impression, because he took a chance and hired me as a studio junior. After a year, the agency noticed the hard work I'd been putting in and took me on full time.

Sush Kelly

Persistence plays a big role and also being open to experiences. I am quite introverted, so not one for networking events, but everyone can play to their strengths so I spend a lot of time on social platforms like Twitter. I think nearly all the pivotal moments in my career can be traced back to either a conversation, opportunity or contact there! One thing that did come from Twitter was making some connections to write a few articles for trade websites and magazines; this helps to build your reputation amongst your peers.

Sylvie Daumal

Thanks to many great people who shared their practices and their experience, I learned a lot from them while attending the conferences (EuroIA, UX Camp Europe, WIAD, IA Summit...), from the books I read and from the Internet (Boxes and Arrows, UXmatters and so many other sources). I also experimented a lot, and failed as much. I'm always learning from my mistakes. This job keeps you modest.

Ross Chapman

It's funny. I try and suggest to upcoming designers that they try and reverse engineer their success, but I totally didn't do that. After leaving University, I went to London to seek my fortune. Fast forward through a number of jobs, a stint at freelancing and understanding what my calling was, I'm now at an agency. How did I get there? I'd say using the Internet, learning what I need and employing persistence.

Nodesign

Having a vision of the future and having a solid cultural and technical background; to propose and defend it without falling into fast-thinking traps.

Amy Parker

I always knew that I wanted to work for myself so after my third job (and only four years of experience), I decided to forge my own path and try my hand at freelancing. That was successful enough that I was able to pull in my partner to work with me full time, which we did for almost ten years. Last year we had the opportunity to work full time with one of our clients to help bring his product vision to life.

Jamie Homer

Lots of hard work. Some mindset changes. Some long hours. Passion and scrupulousness. Progressing through most of the creative roles an agency can offer, has set me in great stead to understand how an agency works both creatively and as a business. It's this commercial understanding that sets the indispensable, must-have creatives, apart from the really good creatives.

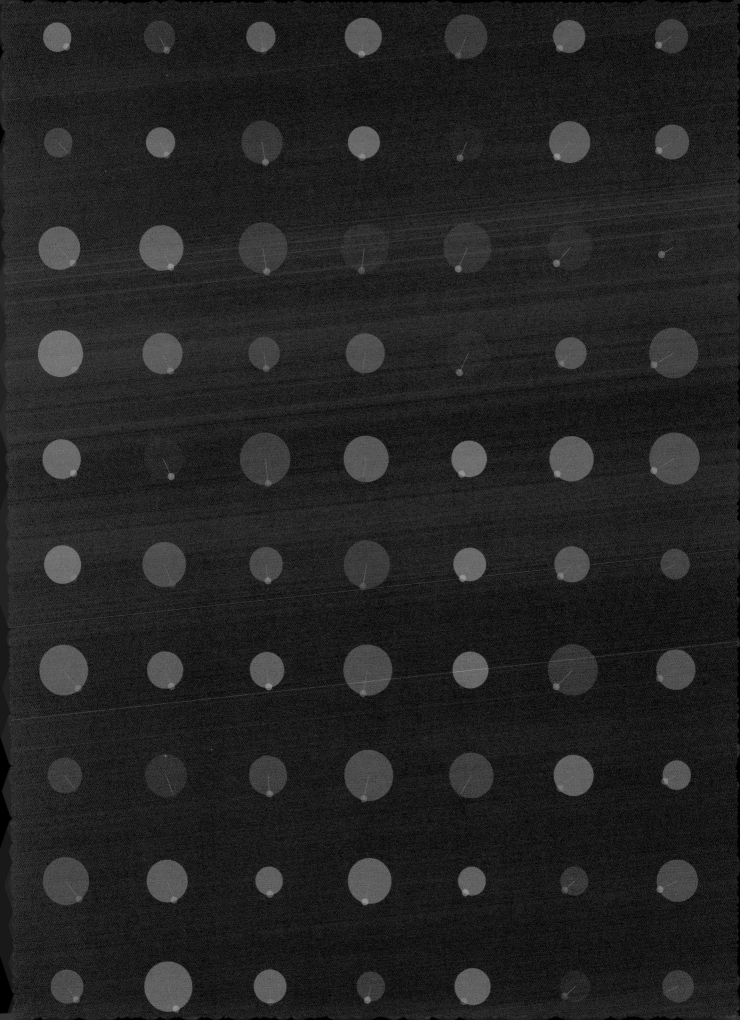

CHAPTER 8:
WHAT'S NEXT?

Over a relatively short period, the role of a graphic designer
has gone from paste-ups to hypertext markup and beyond.
Now the role of a graphic designer has expanded to include
motion, sound, interactivity and whatever's next. While
for many seasoned professionals this transition was
unimaginable at the time when they were students or
junior designers, and they had to retrain rapidly, now this
expansion of knowledge and skills is expected for all people
entering the profession.

Through this chapter, we will explore the implications and
possibilities presented by the ever-expanding range
of technologies and hardware available to designers.
We will examine how these developments are driving new
means of communication for graphic designers and enabling
them to deliver design solutions in an ever-growing number
of formats and platforms, ranging from tablet and mobile,
to smart TV and wearable devices, using static design
to motion graphics and interactive video.

Developments

As technology increases in power and speed, and communication becomes more instantaneous, graphic design outputs have evolved to bring interactive design closer to the viewer. The days of waiting for videos and music to slowly download have now moved forward in leaps and bounds to allow the viewer to interact with video and sound in a wide range of ways never thought of previously. New design companies such as Wirewax and Blippar are taking the next steps in bringing the future to us now.

Wirewax, using its own interactive technology, has allowed shoppers to interact with fashion brands such as Ted Baker. The user watches the video and has the ability to click on clothes they wish to purchase; this click stops the video, and various options emerge: descriptions of the clothing can be read, and colour choices can be made, along with interactive links to purchase the items – all from within the video. This gives new meaning to online shopping, moving away from the traditional online shopping formats of static imagery, and showing the clothes in almost a real world-environment.

Blippar, has blurred the lines between traditional printed media and digital using augmented reality technology. Augmented reality (or AR as it is abbreviated to) allows the designer to add or layer interactive or motion-based content over the top of printed material such as books or magazines. For example, a printed advertisement for a car viewed through a tablet device and the Blippar application (used in conjunction with the tablet's camera) could trigger a video of the car seemingly emerging from the page. This could also contain a spoken narrative, thus giving further information to the viewer. Augmented reality has also been used successfully with children's storybooks to add animation of characters and sound.

Matt Corvis

Antigonish

The images presented in this exhibition illustrate the poem *Antigonish*. Visitors to the exhibit were invited to download an app that added an extra dimension to the printed word. This Augmented Reality app reacted to the images on the wall, and these would change on user's phones to reveal that the story was, in fact, Jekyll and Hyde (Jekyll being the original exhibit, and Hyde being the AR version). This AR experience gave the audience a chance to view the work in a different light, and also to interact with the images as opposed to just observing them.

http://shatteringglass.co.uk/

Devices

Digital platforms and devices have seen an explosion in recent years as companies invest much more into digital solutions and wider formats of hardware that are used within our everyday lives. For example, doorbells with inbuilt cameras alert the homeowner via an app on their smartphone while they are away when a person comes to call, in real time, giving them peace of mind. Technology that checks our internal house rooms and monitors power and climate control have all been added to the long list of devices used and controlled by the user remotely through phone apps.

Tablets and laptops used to vary significantly in processing power, with the laptop user demanding much more energy when working with software on a day-to-day basis. Tablets are now closing the gap – by increasing their power, developing applications that work the same as traditional software, and combining keyboards, the dual functionality of these devices still keep the slim portability of a tablet, but add the power of a computer, giving the user the best of both worlds.

From limited dabblings in the 1980s and mid-1990s, virtual reality (VR) technology has once again seen an emergence and regeneration in interest, with companies such as Samsung and its Samsung Gear VR headset combining VR glasses and the mobile phone. This has led to a plethora of applications fulfilling a virtual 360-degree experience to the wearer in a number of ways, from interactive games to virtual simulations of places and buildings. The adoption of this technology is still in its relatively early stages, but as the technology and hardware develop further, the implications of where VR will take us become an exciting prospect.

Mobile phones, or smartphones as they have become known, have moved from the small screen to almost become tablet devices in themselves; each new generation is becoming increasingly more powerful in its processing power and hardware, with cameras that increase in clarity and professional options with each new generation. The smartphone has become the hybrid device of many, allowing the user to be always connected to the Internet. Applications, such as Microsoft Office 360, even give the user the ability to create and work on basic documents while on the move. With the screen resolution on these new devices, much higher film and video can now be either captured by the device or watched anywhere. This, for the designer, has led to a variety of new design outputs, by developing and designing for the smaller screen.

Luke West
VR Sketches

This page: Utilising VR technology, sketches can be imported to create quick virtual 3D; these sketches can help clients visualise ideas and concepts before they go into production. A designer can then export the files as full 3D models.

Over: Luke West demonstrating Virtual Reality technology.

www.artstation.com/lukewestart

Wearable tech

As the technological hardware of devices reduces in size we begin to see the power of the desktop computer in other tools of communication; mobile phones have developed to such an extent and impacted on our daily lives in such a way that they have now become the norm for keeping communication channels open away from desktop and laptop computers.

Wearable technology was first developed by Chinese companies, creating mobile phone wristwatches in the 2000s, and Apple and Nike's collaboration on the Nike+iPod fitness tracking device gave consumers a way to use their existing technology to keep fit. The initial construction and design of this wearable tech was hampered by the size and bulkiness of the technology itself; it tried to mirror mobile phones in its operation by adding small keyboards for typing in telephone numbers. With the development of touchscreen hardware and the use of apps specifically created for watch technology, this has led to the hardware and design becoming sleeker and much more sympathetic in operation for the end-user.

This technology still retains its main connection to data through the user's mobile phone and a Bluetooth connection to the device – this allows the user to pick up email, track social media, and receive and respond to text messages through voice recognition software. Through a range of apps seen initially developed on a mobile phone, there is now a plethora of applications from GPS tracking and navigation to monitoring the wearer's heart rate and fitness, all developed to move the user away from the mobile phone screen and communicate in new ways through wearable tech.

Some companies have begun the initial steps in taking wearable technology to the next stage, adapting the technology to jewellery such as rings. Better known as 'smart jewellery', this technology is incorporated into the ring by adding a digital processor that can be programmed via a tablet or mobile phone, and uses technology called NFC (Near Field Communication).

NFC technology is already being used in a range of tap-and-go services like Apple Pay, Google Wallet and Samsung Pay. Simply put, it's a method of wireless data transfer that detects and then enables technology in close proximity to communicate without the need for an Internet connection. It is easy, fast and works seamlessly with no other technology involved.

This early use of the technology within rings allows the user to 'digitally tag' information, such as their contact details, automatically unlocks electronic locks built into their home and even controls the settings within other applications built into mobile phones by the swipe of a hand. Although still in its infancy technology-wise, the future of this wearable tech looks promising, with more and more companies investing in bringing to market their own range of jewellery incorporating the technology to some level for both male and females. Rings are the starting point for now, but it has also been successfully used in bracelets, necklaces and even men's cufflinks.

Hedy Hurban

Dervish Sound Dress

The cultural traditions of the Mevlevi Sufis and their metaphysical experience during the turning ritual of the sema performance is the inspiration behind the creation of a garment that emulates sounds by using body movement using wearable technology.

Dervish Sound Dress is outfitted with sensors that trigger musical sounds when the wearer touches the bodice interface or changes gesture or movement.

The wearer is alerted to the sounds through the use of haptics that are sensed on the body. The sensation is similar to when a musician plays an instrument that reverberates, resulting in an immersive relationship that goes further than the auditory.

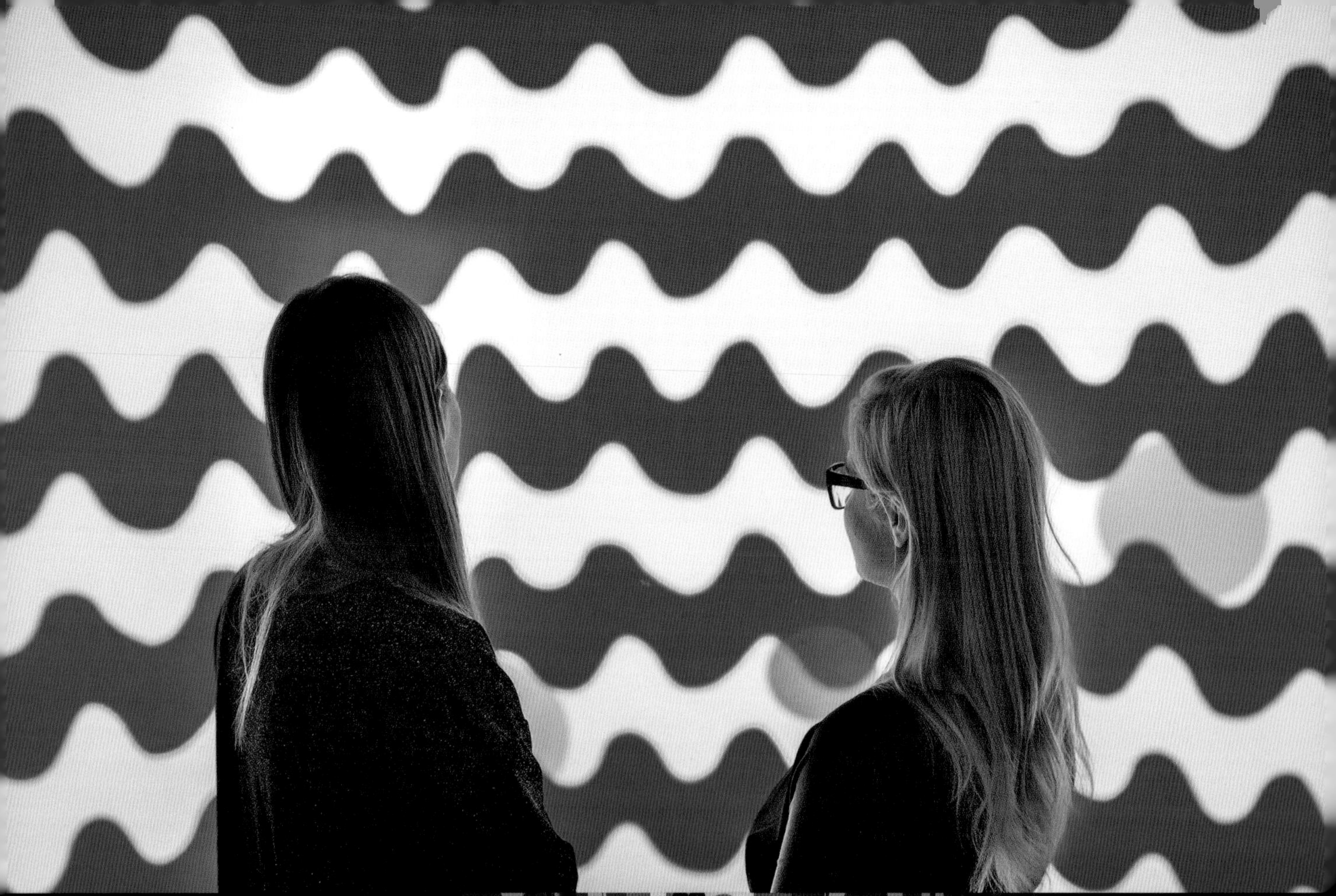

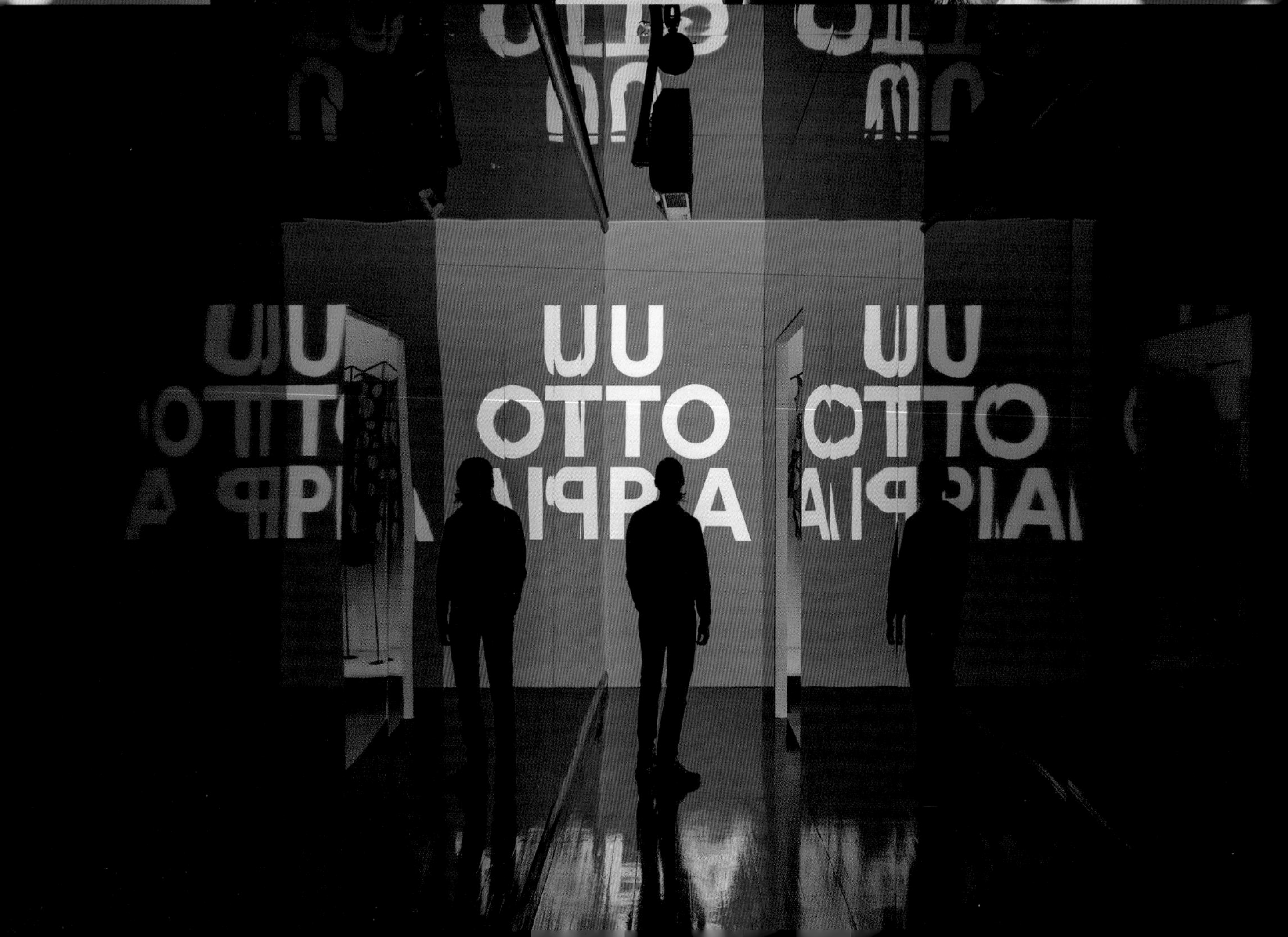
UU
OTTO

Futureproofing

Futureproofing is the process of trying to anticipate developments that will happen in the future; this can be applied to a number of areas, from climate change through to industrial and architectural design and technology.

Futureproofing is not a given science, and if we could all predict the direction of outcomes and products, we would all be millionaires overnight! Futureproofing, in some cases, is relatively new. For example, the digital development of printing with high-speed machines has had a major impact on the traditional offset lithographic industry, where small-run 'jobbing' printing has now moved to the domain of the digital press. Many traditional printing companies did not foresee this development happening until it was too late, and a great number of companies closed down.

Futureproofing for the designer of digital hardware outcomes and products means that over the years a number of new directions have emerged. Motion graphic design, user experience and user interface design, and front-end development are all design directions that have come from emerging technology and visual communication being utilised in a new way. For the designer of today, being current and contemporary means being adaptive and ever-changing when looking to the future. Futureproofing is always being 'aware' of trends, looking at what is happening in technology and what companies are looking to develop. The Internet and its vast range of information is a good starting point in this. Seminars and conferences by leading manufactures of technology, such as Apple and Samsung, give a strong insight into the developments that may be occurring over the next months or years. Even a trip to the local supermarket can give an inkling into what the future may hold with the decline of shopping assistants — self-service checkouts with digital interfaces that navigate the customer through payment all had an initial starting point with a designer. It is all about awareness of visual communication and what will be next.

BOND

Design Museum - Utopia Now exhibition: The Story of Finnish Design

Bond has opened up exciting, new possibilities for the Design Museum, Helsinki, through the use of technology, digital, spatial design and a strong brand identity.

The permanent exhibition, 'Utopia Now: The Story of Finnish Design' highlights the importance of visitor engagement, both inside and outside the museum, through digital engagement. The construction utilises the most recent design trends and is built with a consideration of those currently undiscovered future developments.

The visitor experience is enhanced by clear spatial design, guiding people through the museum's exhibition spaces, as well as through on screen, search-friendly content that complements the exhibit. This, in turn, heightens personal relevance, ensuring that items within the collection are more discoverable, shareable and engaging, while enhancing visitors' ability to provide feedback and join the debate.

www.bond-agency.com/project/design-museum-utopia-now/

Critical discussions: What is technological determinism?

Technological determinism is a theory that is part of a larger field called 'sociology of technology', which studies the relationships between society and tech (from the use of the first tool (e.g. flint) through to Gutenberg's mechanical movable type printing, on to the latest uses of the Internet).

Sociology of technology questions the correlation between technological changes and the development of society: what impact do technologies have on social progress? Does technology shape human activities or do human activities create the need for new technologies? Where do innovations come from?

Coined at the end of the nineteenth century, technological determinism asserts that technology drives society. Informed solely by science, technology is believed to be independent of any contemporaneous contexts (political, cultural, economic) and to determine the development of social values and structures. The advancement of societies would depend only on technological progress.

From this perspective, technology would remove any prerogatives from societies.

Applied to contemporary society, technological determinism, in its most simplistic reading, would mean that the way we think and create is dictated by new technologies: new technologies provide us with a rigid framework that would be impossible to escape from, that would be impossible to exceed (and hack), and that would constrain and limit our creativity. Rather than being considered as a tool that improves workflow, a computer would be seen as an electronic magic box that would generate concepts and ideas; it implies that graphic design outcome aesthetics and functionalities would depend on easily accessible options provided by the machine, hence conditioning designers

to create and produce only what was allowed by programs (applications and software).

It would result in a standardisation of the outcomes – the same aesthetics and functionality whatever the client's brief – and, in the short term, an impoverishment of creativity.

The reality is more complex than suggested above; if it is true that personal computing had a wide and rapid impact on society in general, and on creative industry particularly, it has never been a unilateral relationship. On one hand, by simplifying some fastidious tasks and by relieving humanity from hard physical process, technology modified the labour market (e.g. the disappearance of typesetter jobs) and the structure of society; it has affected human activities from workplace to leisure, and introduced new life priorities (individual property, education, health). However, on the other hand, by creating new uses, appropriating unexpected features (e.g. the development of SMS for mobile phones) and discussing the technology itself, individuals in society, in return, have influenced technology; there is a link of interdependency between society and technology. It may be this dynamic that the designer should underline.

To what extent are your design choices influenced by technological constraints? Who is responsible for the final aesthetics and functionalities of your project: you, the client's competitors or the software engineer? Would you have arranged your page elements differently if you had known about new software features? Would you have used another typeface if you had known how to install a more suitable one? Would you dare to imagine a new feature to your website even if it is not proposed by the software you use/the technology that is proposed to you?

Philipp Frank

METIMOTUS

In his latest project, artist Philipp Frank further explores
the combination of his paintings with 3d projection
mapping. This work is inspired and guided by, the
aesthetics of urban art, and the possibilities afforded
by recent developments in projection mapping.

He explains his concept for the Metimotus installation:

'I wanted to create an inspirational new artwork and find
a connection between the building and its environment.
Therefore I took various natural elements from next to it
(trees, stones, water, colours) and reinterpreted and
abstractly rearranged them. On some spots, you can
find direct links to nature, that can only be seen from
certain angles. It requires the spectator's interaction and
a playful approach to discover them'.

www.philipp-frank.com/

Critical discussions: Internet activism / hacktivism

In the last few years, you may have heard of Edward Snowden or Anonymous in the news. They are internet activists, which means that they use computer and telecommunication technologies to spread their political views. Not every hacker is a hacktivist, but all cyber-resistants use new technology. They fight for human rights, free speech, for the freedom of ideas and information movement and for social changes. For some, hacktivists are considered whistleblower, heroes, like modern Robin Hoods. For others (and among them, their targets: corporations, religious movements, governmental agencies and politicians), their activities are illegal. And, although hacktivists never cause death or significant damage, they are seen by most governments as terrorists who threaten the fragile balance of the political, economic and financial world.

1: When a few raised awareness

Anonymous (2003)
Anonymous is a global online community that performs coordinated attacks on the Web and organise protests such as the Million Mask March, in 2013. When appearing in media, members of Anonymous (called the Anons) wear a mask of Guy Fawkes, in reference to the comics and movie V for Vendetta, where the main character resists a dystopian fascist state.

WikiLeaks (2010)
WikiLeaks was founded in 2006. Its aim is to share knowledge previously reserved for only the minority. WikiLeaks is an international non-profit organisation that shares, on its website, classified information that it believes is relevant to the population. This site is highly controversial because some revelations disclose very sensitive information. WikiLeaks also spreads its findings on Twitter and Facebook, and, for breakthrough revelations on other media: international and

national newspapers, radio and news broadcasts. WikiLeaks gained attention in 2013 when Edward Snowden disclosed the Afghanistan war log. Since then Edward Snowden lives in 'global' illegality and is constrained to hide from authorities.

Aaron Schwartz (1986-2013)
Aaron Schwartz was a young polymath with a very strong sense of ethics. He fought for civic awareness and activism. He was pursued by the US government for having hacked a library and was risking 35 jail sentences.

He developed various technologies to reinforce online communities and speech circulation, such as RSS feeds and SecureDrop that have been used by journalists and hacktivists to share information. He also supported movements such as the Semantic web, the Internet Archive and Open Internet, which he believed were crucial.

2: An opportunity for everyone

Arab Spring (2010-2011)
On a different and more sensitive scale, the Arab Spring illustrates the power of digital communication. Following the Tunisian revolution (2010), with no more digital literacy than anyone else, and mainly using social media to spread messages, citizens of some Middle Eastern countries gathered in the streets to protest against corruption, lack of freedom and for human rights. The role of the Internet was crucial in the coordination of crowd movement.

Although the political consequences of the Arab Spring were local, the movement made citizens from every country more aware of how Internet could help their claims to be coordinated and heard. To a certain extent, Internet, and mainly social media, redistributed the political power. In the decade following the Arab Spring, more popular movements emerged such as Occupy

(2011), #BlackLivesMatter (2013), #metoo (2017) or #ClimateStrike (2019). We have moved from hacktivism, the carefully planned actions of politically aware small groups of digitally skilled people, to popular uprisings, composed of individuals who may not know each other but who have social, political and/or economic issues in common; people who may not have the technical skills to break the global network but who can still disrupt it, by diverting social media from its former goal and transforming it into a massive political weapon. In this way, anyone can use their digital voice as a leverage to change the physical world.

Relying on your knowledge on the economic, financial and political world, what would be the motivations of hacktivism? What and how would you induce social change? What are the pitfalls and benefits of a global network?

Anonymous
A protester wearing the now-familiar Guy Fawkes mask.

Critical discussions: Digital utopia, techno-utopianism

Technological utopianism, an ideology that draws upon the belief that science and technology will help to build an ideal society, was not born with computers. It emerged with the advent of the personal computing era, which started roughly in the 1960s; the term resurfaced during the dotcom bubble of the 1990s.

After the Second World War, people realised that science and technology could bring disaster and horror with sophisticated weapons and centralised means of communication. Many felt that the best way to counter dictatorship and totalitarianism, and fight fallacious ideology, was to create a decentralised source of information and knowledge, a network without hierarchy where all participants are actors, contributors, and spectators.

The American 1960s counterculture brought about an unprecedented movement for freedom; its participants protested against the Vietnam War (intrusion/intervention of the USA into foreign politics), the too-standardised American way of life, the atomic bomb, and they fought for the recognition of women's rights, gay rights, and racial equality. Distrust towards corporations and centralised power, strength in communities and the do-it-yourself ethos were the main driving forces of the movement that was emerging.

Among the hippy generation in San Francisco, not far from Silicon Valley, was Stewart Brand, a man strongly engaged with the counterculture movement and community. He was also the author of the *Whole Earth Catalog* – both a magazine and a directory of self-sufficiency tools, alternate ways of life and ecology. In 1985, Stewart Brand recognised the computer's potential to reinforce and support communities. With Kevin Kelly (future editor of *Wired*), Brand created WELL (Whole Earth 'Lectronic Link) – one of the first virtual communities.

Among the younger generation, there were also hackers; according to *The Jargon File*, a hacker is 'a person who enjoys exploring the details of programmable systems and how to stretch their capabilities, as opposed to most users, who prefer to learn only the minimum necessary' – they looked for a better/alternate way to program computers and to build a better society. Richard Stallman, a student at the MIT, Massachusetts, was one of them. In 1983, he launched the GNU project (General Public License project), supplemented by a formal manifesto and a foundation (Free Software Foundation) in 1985. GNU is a license for free software that guarantees the freedom for the end-user to run, study, share, and modify the software. The free software movement opposes proprietary software as this is a closed system that relies on software patents and excessive use of constraining copyright law. Richard Stallman also popularised the term 'Copyleft', a licensing model that protects authors' moral rights, while allowing users to reappropriate their creation.

The Internet and the Web, thanks to their accessibility and interoperability, brought together like-minded hippies and hackers, artists, activists, and academics on a common ground that fought for the collaborative economy and anti-authoritarianism. Investors were attracted by the possibilities of a global market in the late 1990s, and created a speculative bubble where extensive financial packages and promises for hypothetical gains took over many companies and services. This, as a consequence, altered the Internet's former ideal of a fair, free, and equal society, introducing a capitalist model.

The end of the speculative bubble at the dawn of the 2000s did not erase techno-utopianism but rather marked the rise of technorealism and neo-luddism. Technorealism proposes to re-evaluate the place of technology in our society. Neo-luddism is a movement that mistrusts and refuses the use of technology – its name is taken from the British Luddites, a group who, during the nineteenth century, destroyed the weaving machines as a sign of protest against the automation of their tasks.

What good does technology bring us in the present day? What could be changed with technology that will improve our lives? What legacy remains from the former Internet ideals, and is this model still sustainable?

Digital utopia, techno-utopianism

While recent developments such as wi-fi are hugely useful, many feel these technologies are blocking us from experiencing 'real' life.

Critical discussions: Dark UX / UI: Ethics and design for bad

The term, user experience, (UX) refers to all aspects of the end user's interaction with a company: its services (campaign, website, social media) and its products. User interface (UI) is one part of the customer's whole experience and focuses on the human-artefact interactions in the field of product design, and on human-machine interactions in the field of digital design.

Dark UX, also called dark patterns, are visual tricks included in design interfaces (Dark UI) that lead the user to undertake action(s) that have consequences they may not be aware of (clicking on misdirected links, sharing personal data, answering questions, changing browser settings, buying optional guarantees, services or products, giving access to your social media accounts and your contacts). Dark UX is an invisible twist in the UI, mainly motivated by short-term gains and benefits for businesses, but ultimately it alters the full user's experience: in the longer term, when the end-user is made aware of the tricks and the dishonest practices of the company, their bond to the brand is damaged.

On his website, UX designer Harry Brignull provides a list of the dark pattern categories: Bait and Switch, Disguised Ads, Forced Continuity, Friend Spam, Hidden Costs, Misdirection, Price Comparison Prevention, Privacy Zuckering, Roach Motel, Sneak Into Basket, Trick Questions (Brignull). You have probably been the victim of at least one of these tricks during your journeys through e-commerce sites, or game websites.

Mechanisms
Dark UX draws on our cognitive ability to manage the information workload in an economy where our attention is precious: to spare us cognitive efforts, we build mental patterns that help us to quickly recognise our visual environment,

and to isolate what is important and new from what is expected and reliable. Dark UX gives the interface the appearance of simplicity, order, grouping, and past experience validation as described and recommended in the Gestalt theory [See also: Gestalt, page 30]. But instead of facilitating the end user's goals, it exploits Gestalt features to bring about confusion and annihilate end-user agency, and to impose on them an experience beyond their control, one that has a damaging financial and emotional cost.

Persuasive design, behaviour model and decision-making process
Dark pattern has to be distinguished from persuasive design whose aim is to impact positively on the decision-making process. Persuasive design relies on social influence principles (reciprocity, scarcity, social validation, sympathy/liking, authority and consistency) (Del Gado, 2012), psychological features (such as completeness, positive reinforcement, loss aversion, saving for tomorrow, free appeal and susceptible moment), and the balanced combination of motivation and ability (Fogg).

The designer's role
As a designer, you may not be the one who is going to propose or implement dark patterns. Nevertheless, you will be responsible for poor design decisions and bad user experience. Technology matters not because of what it is, but for what we do with it; for this reason, it could be good for you when you start your career with a clearly defined set of ethics; you should have a set of moral principles that shape how you conduct your professional activity. Being able to refuse deception and short-term gains could be considered as a whole design skill.

Have you experienced dark patterns while using a company's services? Would you be able to deconstruct and analyse it? Do you agree with the company's motivations? As a graphic designer, what other options do you have that might influence the user's behaviour?

What is your first aim when you design for digital? Have you already been asked to design a dishonest interface?

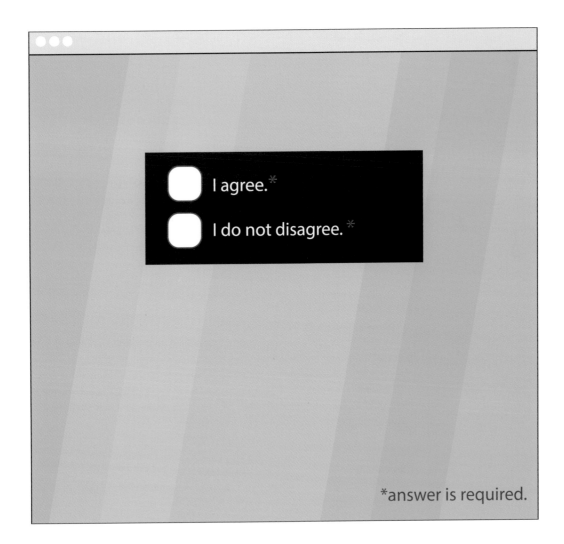

Dark UX
The illusion of positive choice, using convention against the user.

Meet the designers: How do you keep up?

Inayaili de León

I listen to more podcasts than is humanly possible, many about design and Web. I force myself to check Twitter daily; I don't follow a lot of people, but they usually post about relevant things to me, and I save the articles to read later. I also follow a few RSS feeds and check them every weekend. And I subscribe to some newsletters for a more curated view on what's happening in the digital design world. When I have time, I watch interesting conference talks, if I wasn't able to attend the conference in person.

Bruce Lawson

Caffeine.

Dan Hinton

I like to keep engaged in the industry, whether by reading the latest technologies, playing around with some new code, going to talks or teaching. I'd recommend getting involved in your local community – chances are there will be some meetups you can go to.

Ricky Gane

For motion graphics I spend a lot of time watching tutorials on YouTube as that's great for finding a technique to produce a certain style or for inspiration. When starting out I used Skillshare a lot to get me working on real-life projects. The class format really worked for me and I liked the community feel of it. My website inspiration list gets updated all the time, but my two all-time favourites are *From up North* and *Abduzeedo*.

Sush Kelly

It's not easy but you just have to find a way! Luckily of late I have been getting commissions to write tutorials for *NET Magazine* and *Web Designer Magazine* which is great as you get paid to double check your own knowledge. I also try and get involved in local meet ups or events. Volunteering for the Birmingham Design Festival means the opportunity to sit in on talks and a chance to listen to the leaders in design. As mentioned before, in this industry you have to learn almost daily so you kind of get dragged along whether you like it or not!

Sylvie Daumal

Thanks to the great community I belong to and my team, colleagues and clients. Everything is going so fast now that you need others to keep up.

Ross Chapman

Google, social media and conversations. I don't really go to many conferences or events, but I do meet people for coffee and learn from them. The podcast that I started a year ago has encouraged me to talk to people I really want to learn from.

I also experiment to learn. Part of running a business within a business means that I get to do a range of activities, from having conversations on LinkedIn, to calls with potential prospects, to running workshops and delivering backlogs and reports.

Nodesign

We never get bored. Every new project is an opportunity to dive into a topic. Good design is a necessary tool to prevent the world from falling apart.

Amy Parker

I go back and forth between phases of intensive browsing (mostly Dribbble, Instagram, and my favourite designers' portfolios) and trying to focus on my work without being influenced too much by anything. When I get to a specific problem that I'm stuck on though, I try to find something comparable, study it, analyse it, and try to find the underlying principles, then I take those learnings back to the problem I'm trying to solve.

Jamie Homer

With the Internet, it's never been easier to stay current with both your skills and creative inspiration! Web and digital technology have made it incredibly easy to get an endless stream of brilliant inspiration at no cost – I am thinking specifically of sites like Pinterest and Dribbble. There are also loads of great video tutorials online about getting the most out of your software, some of which are paid but well worth the money – such as Lynda.com and Udemy.

Further reading

Airey, D. (2012), *Work for Money, Design for Love: Answers to the Most Frequently Asked Questions About Starting and Running a Successful Design Business (Voices That Matter)*, New Riders.

de Soto, D. (2014), *Know Your Onions: Graphic Design: How to Think Like a Creative, Act Like a Businessman and Design Like a God*, Bis Publishers.

de Soto, D. (2014), *Know Your Onions: Web Design: Jet Propel Yourself into the Driving Seat of a Top-Class Web Designer and Hurtle towards Creative Stardom*, Bis Publishers.

de Soto, D. (2014), *What to Put in Your Portfolio and Get a Job: Graphic Design*, Articul8 Publishing.

Glei, J. K. & 99U (2013), *Manage Your Day-to-Day: Build Your Routine, Find Your Focus, and Sharpen Your Creative Mind (The 99U Book Series)*, Amazon Publishing.

Glei, J. K. & 99U (2013), *Maximize Your Potential: Grow Your Expertise, Take Bold Risks & Build an Incredible Career (The 99U Book Series)*, Amazon Publishing.

Glei, J. K. & 99U (2014), *Make Your Mark: The Creative's Guide to Building a Business with Impact (The 99U Book Series)*, Amazon Publishing.

NESTA (Editor) (2011), *Launch Your Own Successful Creative Business: Creative Enterprise Toolkit*, 3rd Revised Edition, NESTA.
[See also: www.nesta.org.uk/publications/creative-enterprise-toolkit]

Shaughnessy, A. & Brook, T. (2009), *Studio Culture: The Secret Life of the Graphic Design Studio*, Unit Editions.

Stone, T. (2010), *Managing the Design Process, Volume 1: Concept Development*, Rockport.

Ambrose, G. & Aono-Billson, N. (2010), Basics Graphic Design 01: Approach and Language, AVA Publishing.

Barnard, M. (2005), Graphic Design as Communication, Routledge.

Bergström, B. (2009), *Essentials of Visual Communication*, Laurence King.

Chandler, D. (2007), Semiotics: The Basics, Routledge.

Crow, D. (2010), *Visible Signs: An Introduction to Semiotics in the Visual Arts*, 2nd edition, AVA Publishing.

Ingledew, J. (2011), *The A - Z of Visual Ideas: How to Solve any Creative Brief*, Laurence King.

Leonard, N. & Ambrose G. (2012), *Basics Graphic Design 02: Design Research: Investigation for successful creative solutions*, AVA Publishing.

Leonard, N. & Ambrose G. (2012), *Basics Graphic Design 03: Idea Generation*, AVA Publishing.

Lupton, E. (2011), *Graphic Design Thinking: Beyond Brainstorming (Design Briefs)*, Princeton Architectural Press.

Noble, I. & Bestley, R. (2011), *Visual Research: An Introduction to Research Methodologies in Graphic Design*, AVA Publishing.

Marxism and the information economy

Casilli, A. (2017), *Digital Labour Studies Go Global: Toward a Digital Decolonial Turn. International Journal of Communication, 11, Special Section "Global Digital Culture":* 3934–3954. Available at: http://ijoc.org/index.php/ijoc/article/viewFile/6349/2149

Jenkins, H. (2005). *Confronting the Challenges of Participatory Culture: Media Education for the 21st Century.* Available at: https://www.macfound.org/media/article_pdfs/JENKINS_WHITE_PAPER.PDF

Marx, K and Engels, F. (1848), *The Communist Manifesto.* Available at: http://www.gutenberg.org/ebooks/61

Mauss, M. (1925), *The Gift, London: Cohen & West Ltd*. Available at : https://monoskop.org/images/a/ae/Mauss_Marcel_The_Gift_The_Form_and_Functions_of_Exchange_in_Archaic_Societies_1966.pdf

Web 3.0: Semantic Web

https://www.w3.org/standards/semanticweb/

Open Internet and Net neutrality

Wu, T., (2011), *The Master Switch: The Rise and Fall of Information Empires*, London: Atlantic Books.

Art on/with the Internet

Blais, J. and Ippolito, J. (2006), *At the Edge of Art*, London: Thames and Hudson Ltd.

Greene, R. (2004), *Internet art*, London: Thames and Hudson Ltd.

Ricardo, F. (2009), *Literary art in digital performance*, London: Bloomsbury.

Colson, R., (2007), *The Fundamentals of Digital Art*, London: Bloomsbury.

Feminism and intersectionality

Universities UK. (2015), *Pattern and trends in UK Higher Education 2015*. Available at: http://www.universitiesuk.ac.uk/policy-and-analysis/reports/Documents/2015/patterns-and-trends-2015.pdf (Accessed 16th April 2017).

Breuer, G. and Meer, J. (2012), *Women in Graphic Design 1890-2012*, Berlin: Jovis Verlag.

De Grazia, V. (1996), *The Sex of Things: Gender and Consumption in Historical Perspective*, Berkeley, CA: University of California Press.

Crenshaw, K. (2017), *On Intersectionality: Essential Writings*, New-York: The New Press.

Digital utopia, techno-utopianism

Bush, V. (1945) *As we may think*. Available at: http://web.mit.edu/STS.035/www/PDFs/think.pdf

Barbrook, R. and and Andy Cameron A. (1995), Available at: http://www.metamute.org/editorial/articles/californian-ideology

Berners Lee, T. (1989), *Information Management: A proposal*. Available at : https://www.w3.org/History/1989/proposal.html

McLuhan, M. (2008), *The medium is the massage*, London: Penguin

Nelson, T. (1974) *Computer Lib/Dream machine in New Media Reader* (2003), Ed.. Wardrip-fruin, N. Boston MA: MIT Press, pp. 301-338. Available at: http://www.newmediareader.com/book_samples/nmr-21-nelson.pdf

Stallman, R. *General Public License project*. Available at: https://www.gnu.org/

Turner, F. (2006), *From Counterculture to Cyberculture: Stewart Brand, the Whole Earth Network, and the Rise of Digital Utopianism*, Chicago, IL: University of Chicago Press.

Dark UX/UI: Ethics and design for bad

Brignull, H. *Dark Patterns*, Available at: https://darkpatterns.org/

Del Gado, E. (2012). *Persuasion in Design*, Available at: https://www.slideshare.net/wearesigma/persuasion-in-design

Fogg, B.J. *What Causes Behavior Change?*, Available at: http://www.behaviormodel.org/

Nielsen, J. (1995), *10 Usability Heuristics for User Interface Design*. Available at: https://www.nngroup.com/articles/ten-usability-heuristics/

See also: #darkpattern on Twitter

For more, see: www.wdgd.co.uk

Index

Page locators in italics refer
to illustrations.

Acknowledgements

The authors would like to thank Louise Baird-Smith, Sophie Tann and Leafy Cummins.

Andy would like to thank Wendy and his family.

Frédérique would like to thank Garrett, Ripley and Magali for their patience and curiosity.

Neil would like to thank Sarah, Mary, Phil and Rachel Leonard, Katie and Manuel Cruz, Paul Allen, Alex Bradbeer, Rich Hurst, Jamie Homer, John Fry, the team at PCA, Jamie Steane, and Tom May, for their support and encouragement.

The authors dedicate this text to all of the students and educators we have worked with.

Thank you to our intervewees:
Inayaili de León: www.yaili.com/
Bruce Lawson: www.brucelawson.co.uk/
Dan Hinton: www.pixelfish.co.uk/
Ricky Gane: www.rickygane.co.uk/
Sush Kelly: www.sushkelly.co.uk/
Sylvie Daumal: www.wedigital.garden/
Ross Chapman: www.rosschapman.com/
Nodesign: www.nodesign.net/
Amy Parker: www.foredesign.co/
Jamie Homer: www.jamiehomer.co.uk/

Image Credits

p 3, 73 — BANK Associates: www.bankassociates.de/
p 7 — Amy Parker: www.amyhparker.com/
P 8, 9 — Planning Unit: www.planningunit.co.uk/
p 37 — Bunch Design: www.bunchdesign.com/
p 39 — Alexandro Valcarcel: www.behance.net/avalcarcel
p 41 — Pixelfish: www.pixelfish.co.uk/
p 52, 57 — wedigital.garden: www.wedigital.garden/
p 63, 75 — Jamie Homer: www.jamiehomer.co.uk/
p 66, 67 — Ross Chapman: www.rosschapman.com/
p 68-71 — Niccolò Miranda: www.niccolomiranda.com/
p 79 — Sheida Pourian: www.behance.net/popisheida/
p 100-101 — Till Nagel and Benedikt Groß: www.tillnagel.com/
p 111 — Christopher Pietsch: www.uclab.fh-potsdam.de/cf/
p 119-121 — Tai Chen: www.behance.net/ChenHueiTai/
p 153 — Neil Leonard: www.neilrobertleonard.co.uk/
p 162-163, 165 — Panic Studio: www.panicstudio.tv/
p 166 — BluBlu Studios: www.blublustudios.com/
p 171 — Garrett Lynch IRL: www.asquare.org/
p 179, 199 — Bond Agency: www.bond-agency.com/
p 181, 185 — AGGRESSIVE: www.aggressive.tv/
p 192-193 — Matt Corvis: http://shatteringglass.co.uk/
p 194-195 — Luke West: www.artstation.com/lukewestart/
p 197 — Hedy Hurban
p 201 — Philipp Frank: www.philipp-frank.com/